M000074285

vSphere 4.0 Quick Start Guide

ISBN: 1-4392-6345-0

EAN: 978-1-4392-6345-7

Foreword

About a year ago I was approached by some of the folks in the VMware community that wanted to write a new "Quick Start" guide for vSphere. Why they approached me I wasn't sure of immediately, but later realized they thought they needed my permission. As if I owned the concept of a Quick Start guide for VMware since I worked on the first one while at RapidApp. I told them that the RapidApp Quick Start guide fell out from a bunch of technical guys working together to document the 'new' way to do things in ESX 3.0 and we were not planning on doing another one so they should knock their socks off. Secretly I had hoped someone would take the time to create a new guide but I knew I no longer had the cycles to do so.

The results of this group's efforts is what you are holding in your hand or reading on your screen now. The authors of this guide (Thomas, Duncan, Dave, Stuart, Alan and Bernie) have done an outstanding job in continuing what we tried to accomplish with the first guide: no nonsense, concise step by step directions, straight to the point descriptions / 'how to's' to allow you to quickly get up to speed on daily tasks in vSphere. It is also nice to see that the warning flags and 'gotchas' have been carried over from the original.

The amount of work these guys have put into this book is probably very under appreciated. Most of these 'how to's' are only a page or so long (in small font and on small pages!). But what is not seen are the hours spent setting up a lab, getting the supporting software, testing the steps and then documenting them. Any given 'how to' may take hours to create. As I said, I appreciate their effort, and my hat is off to them.

With all of this said, and my endless blabbering about how hard they worked on this book finished, I think you will find this book useful as a daily companion. My reading of it even alerted me to a couple of things I had missed previously, so for that I am grateful to the authors.

Thomas, Duncan, Dave, Stuart, Alan and Bernie (wow, that's a lot of guys), thanks for the excellent resource. And thank you for carrying on the tradition we have in our community of getting solid, useful, technical information out at what is essentially no profit to the authors that have put in so much work.

Ron Oglesby

Introduction

Months ago I shared an idea on Twitter about starting a "super blog". This "super blog" should have contained the top articles of some of the best VMware or virtualization bloggers around. I asked myself what the added value would be and came to the conclusion that there already were many "super blogs" around. Although the "super blog" idea died a slow death the urge to collaborate with others on a challenging project still lived on.

This is when the idea of a book series was born. The original idea was to publish a series of short topics with each book limited to 150 pages, sold at a minimum price and completely "diy". This book (and hopefully the rest of the following books) is written by six well known VMware community members. When we started outlining our first book Ron Oglesby gave us the opportunity to rewrite the Quick Start Guide he and his team at RapidApp published in March 2007. We all agreed that this would be a good start of the series. Thanks again Ron! Of course this book will exceed the limit we agreed on of 150 pages, but it is worth it.

I would like to quote from Ron's original version to introduce this guide. "In computing there are always at least two ways to do any task, and more often than not more than that." In most of the sections of this guide we have only shown a single answer for any particular problem. While there may be 50 ways to delete a certain file, we felt it best to keep it simple and show the one way that we tested on a base 4.0 build. We apologize if we happened to miss a cool solution in these pages. Let us know about it and we can add it in for the next revision.

I hope you will enjoy reading it as much as we did writing it. Thanks for your support.

Duncan Epping

The team would like to say thanks to our (technical) editors Paul Nothard(VMware), Chad Sakac(EMC) and Daniel Martushev. We also would like to thank the VMware forum participants and moderators that supplied a constant stream of questions, answers, and really innovative solutions. Some of the answers in this guide have been derived from forum responses and have been validated or improved by our team.

Disclaimer/Common sense

The processes and procedures laid out in this guide were written using VMware vSphere 4.0. All procedures and steps in this guide should be tested in a lab environment PRIOR to being used in production. Some configurations and procedures in the guide can affect major subsystems in your vSphere infrastructure (like storage or networking) and could cause adverse effects or system outages if they are not done correctly.

We make no warranties (written or implied) on the steps or procedures in this guide. When using procedures in this guide, you do so at your own risk.

Table of Contents

Major differences of ESX 3.X and vSphere 4.0

With the release of VMware vSphere 4.0, there are a lot of new features and architectural changes. Some of the new features and changes are minor, but the majority of them are significant. Covered below are some of the changes that you may need to know when you are deploying vSphere in your environment.

Notable architectural changes

The first architectural change that you will notice is vNetwork Distributed Switches. This is the next generation virtual networking solution. The vDS can span multiple hosts which enables you to reduce maintenance activities. In short, you can configure vSwitches on the cluster level instead of per host. This new architecture is also the foundation for third-party distributed vSwitches. The first of these is the Cisco Nexus 1000v which is already available for use.

The next new change is the Pluggable Storage Architecture (PSA). The PSA is an open modular framework that enables third-party storage multipathing solutions for workload balancing and high availability. A good example of a third-party solution is EMC's Powerpath/VE which will automate and optimize server, storage and path utilization. The new architecture consists of several components. These components can be replaced individually by third-party modules or by an all in one multipathing plugin.

The last but definitely not least notable change is VMware VMsafe. VMware VMsafe is a new technology that leverages the properties of vSphere to protect virtual machines. The VMware VMsafe API enables partners to develop security related products. It provides transparency into the memory, CPU, disk and I/O systems of the virtual machine, and monitors every aspect of the execution of the system. This can provide a totally new approach for anti-virus solutions or firewalling for instance.

Notable new features

VMware Fault Tolerance (FT) is one of the most talked about new features, which provides stateful fail-over on a per virtual machine basis. There is no need to introduce it because everyone has seen the demos or tried it by now.

A new feature that will make the life of many system administrators much easier is host profiles. Host profiles enable the user to configure a host via a policy. You can also use these policies to maintain consistency in your virtual environment.

In ESX 4.0 you no longer need to resort to extending VMFS volumes when a volume runs out of disk space. The chances of running out of disk space without noticing have also been reduced by the added storage views, reports and alarms. One of the reasons these views, reports and alarms have been added is "thin provisioning". This new GUI feature will enable you to quickly deploy virtual machines with a minimal disk size.

Where ESX 3.0 and vCenter 2.0 had Distributed Resource Scheduling (DRS) as one of the most compelling features, vSphere has a fully supported version of Distributed Power Management (DPM). Wake On LAN, IPMI or iLO can be used to wake up any host when needed. When we are talking about TCO/ROI this is one of the features that can and will make a real difference.

Obviously the feature list for vSphere 4.0 is huge and these are just some of the key changes we see that people are excited about. From the geek perspective, we also found the following "less pumped" features very cool and these features will improve usability and manageability:

- Improved centralized licensing functionality

- Up to eight virtual processors in a virtual machine (VM)

- Improvements to esxtop, which allow for more granularity (such as the ability to determine which vmnic a VM is using!)

- Up to 255GB of RAM per VM

- Additional esxcfg-* commands.

- Per VMFS volume resignaturing

- Consolidated backup API

- Better granularity of security within vCenter (including datastores!)

- Granular permissions at the network and datastore level

- HA Maintenance mode

- Improved HA admission control

- VMkernel protection

- New hardware/drivers such as VMXNET Generation 3, Paravirtualized SCSI (PVSCSI)

- Enhanced host power management

- iSCSI software initiator improvements

- Jumbo frame support for 1Gb and 10Gb NICs

So what should I set up first?

It mainly depends on two things: if you will be using a physical or virtual vCenter server and whether or not your host is (or will be) SAN-attached.

If your host is standalone, go ahead and start the install. Be sure to check back with this guide if you have a question.

If your host will be part of a vCenter Server managed environment and SAN-attached, then you should probably first build your vCenter Server, then install ESX, and then deal with SAN storage. Below is a chronological approach to implementing your Virtual Infrastructure when your vCenter server is physical:

1. Configure your vCenter Server implementation

2. Install and configure your ESX hosts

3. Attach hosts to your SAN

4. Migrate your physical servers or create new VMs.

If you planned for your vCenter server to be a virtual machine you will need to setup at least one ESX host or install it on VMware Workstation and use VMware Converter to import it into your virtual environment.

vCenter

With all the changes to 4.0, including the new licensing model, we felt that vCenter plays a key role in the new architecture and deserved the first section in the guide. In this section of the guide you will see some basic concepts for the vCenter server, new features and some interesting ways to configure and upgrade the database vCenter is using.

What are the requirements for a vCenter server?

Your vCenter server should be one of the first things that you set up. As outlined by the Installation and Upgrade Guide, the requirements for setting up vCenter are:

- A physical or virtual machine
- 2 CPU Cores
- 2.0GHz or higher Intel or AMD x86 processor
- 3GB RAM minimum memory
- 2GB disk storage
- 10/100 Ethernet adapter minimum, Gigabit is recommended.

For the operating system, you'll need:

- Windows 2000 SP4, with Update Rollup 1
- Windows XP Pro
- Windows 2003, all releases
- Windows 2008, all releases except Datacenter 64-bit

And finally for the database, you should use:

- Microsoft SQL Server 2005/2008
- Oracle 10g, 11g

 SQL Server Express is supported, but realistically, you shouldn't consider this as an option for anything other than demonstrations or for building a small lab.

With the above requirements, a vCenter server can support 20 concurrent clients (people connected via the vSphere Client), 50 ESX Server hosts, and over 250 virtual machines. A quad-processor vCenter

server with 8GB RAM can scale to 50 concurrent
client connections, 300 ESX Server hosts, and over
3000 virtual machines.

Can my vCenter server be a Virtual Machine?

There is no reason why your vCenter server can't be a virtual machine as
long as it meets the requirements and gets the resources it needs. The
environment (and especially HA) will continue to function if the host
where the vCenter server resides becomes unavailable. The drawback to
doing this is that if there is an unusual problem (e.g., where your host
that's hosting vCenter is having issues, or where the VM is not easily
recovered), you will not have your vCenter server to
manage/troubleshoot the environment. Of course you can always use
your vSphere Client directly connected to a host in these situations.

We recommend a virtual vCenter server in any environment as it will
make your vCenter server instantly highly available and it eases disaster
recovery as it can be cloned with just a few steps.

However, when virtualizing vCenter remember a couple of things:

1. Disable DRS(Change Automation Level!) for your vCenter
   VM and make sure to document where the vCenter server is
   located (Our suggestion would be the first ESX host.)

2. Enable HA for the vCenter server, and set the startup
   priority to high

3. Make sure the vCenter server gets enough resources by
   setting the shares "high", and maybe even set reservations

4. Make sure vCenter starts up automatically when a power cut
   occurs (Configuration, Virtual Machine Startup and
   Shutdown)

5. Make sure other services and servers that vCenter relies on
   are also starting automatically, with a high priority and in the
   correct order like:

   a. Active Directory

   b. DNS

   c. SQL

If your vCenter database is also virtual, setting an affinity rule to keep
both virtual machines on the same host will increase performance. All
network traffic will remain inside the host.

High Availability for vCenter Server

VMware, in partnership with The Neverfail Group, released a product called VMware vCenter Heartbeat. Version 5.5 Update 1 was the first version to support vCenter Server 4.0. This product goes far beyond just simple clustering as it adds several key features you need for High Availability:

- Monitors all of the various components of vCenter and its plug-ins, like Update Manager.

- Performs replication of the database (Local or Remote databases are supported)

- Allows for automated or manual failover of services in the event of a disaster or disruption.

In many instances, High Availability for your vCenter server isn't necessary. While a nice to have, it's not always a requirement. Likewise, clustering doesn't always guarantee availability, as it protects from hardware failure but not from data corruption or a lost LUN from a SAN array, etc.

The best bet is to ensure the following:

- Provide a highly available database environment for vCenter (like clustering the DB—if not the server—which is just a front end for the DB).

- Create (and validate) steps for recovering your vCenter server if it fails, while still retaining the original database.

- Create a recovery process for the database and a solid backup and QA of the DB every so often.

- Test-run your vCenter server as a VM within an HA cluster of numerous hosts and keep the DB on a separate database cluster.

Even if the vCenter server isn't available, you still have the following:

- Licenses are good for 14 days, when using the vCenter 2.5 Licensing mechanism for backwards compatibility. When using the vCenter 4.0 licensing mechanism licenses are centrally managed but stored on the host.

- Virtual machines will continue to function.

- HA will continue to work.

- Admins will not be able to make changes, but the VMs will continue to function as normal.

- You will still have the option to connect directly to a host with the vSphere client or if and when enabled use web access.

Installing and using the vSphere Client

The vSphere Client is the client that is used to communicate to both a vSphere 4 ESX Server and vCenter 4.0. It is a Microsoft Windows application and requires Microsoft .NET Framework 3.0 SP1. The installation software is found in one of three places: installed from vCenter installation media, downloaded from a ESX Server with a web browser, or downloaded from vCenter 4.0 Server. To download the software, you simply point a web browser at either an ESX Server or the vCenter server, download the executable to your workstation, and install.

The installation process follows a standard procedure, asking you to accept the licensing agreement and identify the installation directory for the vSphere Client. If the Microsoft .NET Framework 3.0 SP1 is not installed, it will be installed for you as part of the client installation process. Typically, a reboot is not required after installation is complete.

The vSphere Client is used to manage and configure the vSphere 4 ESX Server and vCenter Server. From the vSphere Client you can create/remove virtual machines and add/remove hosts to the VC environment. In addition, you can create/remove Resource Groups, VMware DRS Clusters, and VMware HA Clusters. You can also monitor the performance of your virtual machines, hosts resource groups, and clusters.

To connect to an ESX Server directly, put the host name or IP address in the "server" box in the first window of the vSphere Client. For user name and password you will need to use a local account on the ESX server (like root, which works even though you can't use it for SSH by default).

To connect to a vCenter server just place the vCenter server's IP address or host name into the 'Server' box in the authentication window. But, when connecting to vCenter, you need to use a Windows account to log in.

Do not forget to install appropriate security patches for Microsoft's .NET Framework 3.0 SP1

You must have access to the ESX hosts and/or vCenter environment to use the Virtual Infrastructure client.

What happens if my licensing server is down?

Licenses are good for 14 days, after which you won't be able to do certain things, such as:

- Power on virtual machines
- Add an ESX host
- Move an ESX Server in/out of a DRS-HA cluster
- Start VMotion
- DRS cluster load-balancing
- Restart VMs
- Add or remove license keys
- Upgrade.

As long as your hosts refresh their licenses sometime during the 14 days, you should be good to go. However, it can be quite complicated if your vCenter and license server is a VM and on a host with an expired license.

 Keep in mind that this is only applicable when the vCenter 2.5 Licensing server is used for backwards compatibility.

PowerCLI Example

PowerCLI can not help in this situation but PowerShell itself can be used to monitor the License service and email a set email address if the license server is unavailable, the following script will allow you to do this and should be setup as a scheduled windows task.

Cmdlets
Get-View

Related Cmdlets
Get-VIObjectByVIView

EXAMPLE 1:
Monitors the License server service and emails if the service is not running:

```
Function EmailAlert () {
        $smtpServer = "mysmtpserver.com"

        $msg = new-object Net.Mail.MailMessage
        $smtp = new-object Net.Mail.SmtpClient($smtpServer)

        $msg.From= "me@mydomain.com"
```

```
        $msg.To.Add("me@mydomain.com")
        $msg.Subject= "VMware License Server Check"
        $msg.Body= "The VMware license Server service is not
in a running state, please investigate."

        $smtp.Send($msg)
}

$ServiceInstance = Get-View ServiceInstance
$LicenseMan = Get-View $ServiceInstance.Content.LicenseManager

$LicenseServer =
(($LicenseMan.Source.LicenseServer).split('@'))[1]
$State = get-wmiobject win32_service -ComputerName
$LicenseServer -filter "Name='VMware License Server'" |Select
State

if ($State.State-ne "Running"){
EmailAlert
}
```

Configuring the database on Microsoft SQL Server for vCenter

Microsoft SQL Server 2005/2008 is one of the supported database formats for vCenter. It's also much more scalable and robust than SQL 2005 Express, as well as being easy to set up, and the most commonly used database for vCenter implementations (lets face it, it's a Microsoft world).

Before installing vCenter, you should check the following:

- Although the database can be relatively small, you should also ensure that your SQL server is sized appropriately. If it's a shared resource, check the current memory and processor utilization by running Performance Monitor.

- Set up your database so it is backed up nightly or weekly. At a minimum, set the maintenance wizard to back up each night.

- Ensure you rotate transaction logs or back them up to reduce the overall size of the vCenter database.

- For authentication, use SQL Server authentication; it's faster and easier to maintain and you don't have to worry about someone deleting, disabling or resetting the password of your vCenter account.

- Ensure the sa password (as well as the other passwords) is strong. None of them should be blank.

- On a physical server, load the operating system and SQL Server application on a mirrored drive; store the log file on a mirrored drive or RAID 1; and separate the data on a RAID 5 array.

To set up a new database:

1. Connect to your MS SQL Server using Enterprise Manager (you can also log on locally and open it).

2. If your SQL Server isn't registered, then go ahead and right-click on SQL Server Group and then select New SQL Server Registration.

3. Expand the SQL Server object and then right-click on Databases to create a new database.

4. Name the database (use something easy to identify, like vCenter) and select the appropriate paths for the data files and transaction logs.

5. Expand the security object and then right-click on Logins. Create a new login.

6. Set the login to use SQL Server authentication.

7. Set a strong password.

8. Set the default database to one you just created.

9. On the Database Access tab, check "permit" for the new database and for database roll, then check db_owner.

Once complete, expand the Maintenance object and then right-click Backup. Your specific backup plan will depend on what you have available to back up to and your maintenance window.

 Although most Microsoft 'best practices' recommend using Windows Authentication for access, these generally are linked to SQL applications for end users and not necessarily service accounts. SQL Server logins are faster and the account is less likely to be locked out due to a forced password policy GPO.

Adding an ESX 4.x host to vCenter

In order to manage your ESX host using vCenter, you need to add it to the vCenter console. This process (basically) connects to the host server, then adds a local user (vpxuser) that will act as a service account for VC instructions. To add the host you'll need to connect to the vCenter server using the vSphere Client. Once in the vSphere Client (if you haven't done so already) make a new datacenter (DC) by right-clicking on Hosts & Clusters. Name the DC for the location the host is located in (when adding more hosts from this datacenter, just repeat the steps below).

After the datacenter is created, right-click on the datacenter object and select Add Host.

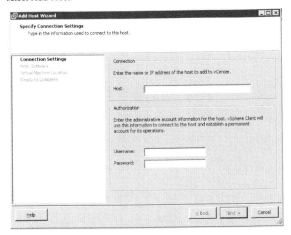

Enter your host's FQDN (if you've added an entry for it in your DNS server) or the IP address along with root for the user name and root's password. This will allow the creation of the service account that is used for future authentication.

Adding hosts to vCenter will not affect the VMs that are running on the hosts.

 If your host is on the opposite side of a firewall or device that is doing port filtering (like an isolated mgmt network), ensure that TCP port 902 is open from the vCenter server to the managed hosts.

PowerCLI Example

The following shows how PowerCLI can be used to add a host into vCenter:

```
Cmdlets
Get-Cluster
```

```
Get-VMHost
```

Related Cmdlets
```
Move-Cluster
New-Cluster
Remove-Cluster
Set-Cluster
```

EXAMPLE 1:
Adds a new host named newESXhost.mydomain.com to the Production Datacenter:

```
Add-VMHost "NewESXhost.mydomain.com " -Location (Get-
Datacenter Production) -User root -Password MyPass
```

Can I add my ESX 2.x/3.x host to my vCenter 4.0 server?

Yes, you can use vCenter 4.0 to "manage" your 2.x & 3.x hosts. You should keep in mind that:

- For ESX 2.x, some functionality such as host configuration and licensing, won't be available and you'll still have to use the MUI.

- ESX 2.x hosts cannot be a part of a resource pool, nor can its VMs be configured to use HA.

- Ensuring that your vCenter server has enough licenses to cover the ESX 2.x & 3.x hosts.

- Only one instance, regardless of the vCenter version can manage an ESX host.

- Advanced features, such as Fault Tolerance or Host Profiles only work on ESX 4 hosts.

 While you can VMotion VMs to other ESX 2.x hosts, you will not be able to VMotion them to the 3.x or 4.x hosts or vice versa. ESX 3.x VMs can be VMotioned to ESX 4.x, but cannot go from ESX 4.x to ESX 3.x if you upgrade the virtual hardware.

Setting up VMotion

Enabling VMotion is done by adding a VMkernel port group to a virtual switch and ensuring that VMotion is configured under the licensed options. We assume you can handle the licensing part (see Licensing a Host), so for the VMkernel port you will need to have an IP address and (it's highly recommended that you use gigabit) a dedicated network connection. Often, organizations will even create a new VLAN or use an existing backup or management VLAN to help isolate the traffic caused by VMotion. It can be made non-routable to allow for total segregation which is sometimes required for compliance purposes.

1. Log into your ESX host or vCenter using the vSphere Client.

2. Highlight the host and then select the Configuration tab.

3. Under the Hardware box in the center of the screen, select Networking and then to the right, select Add Networking.

4. Choose VMkernel as the connection type.

5. On the next screen, select the physical network interfaces to bond to.

6. On the Connection Settings screen, be sure to check the box "Use this port group for VMotion" and then enter the IP address and subnet mask.

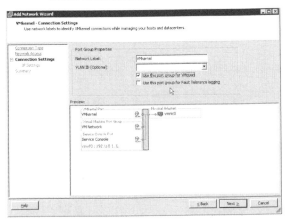

7. Confirm your settings and then click Finish.

8. If you haven't already done so, you'll be prompted to add a default gateway for the VMkernel.

 This section assumes that you have met the other requirements for VMotion, such as: Hosts configured in a like manner, shared storage seen by all clustered hosts, etc.

PowerCLI Example

The following shows how PowerCLI can be used to add a VMKernel vswitch and portgroup and enable VMotion for this:

Cmdlets
```
New-VirtualSwitch
New-VirtualPortGroup
New-VMHostNetworkAdapter
```

Related Cmdlets
```
Get-VirtualSwitch
Remove-VirtualPortGroup
Set-VirtualPortGroup
Get-VirtualPortGroupRemove-VMHostNetworkAdapter
Set-VMHostNetworkAdapter
```

EXAMPLE 1:
Adds a new VMotion portgroup to newESXhost.mydomain.com:

```
$NewSwitch = New-VirtualSwitch -VMHost
"MyESXHost.mydomain.com" -Name "vSwitch1" -Nic vmnic1
New-VirtualPortGroup -Name vmkernel -VirtualSwitch $NewSwitch
New-VMHostNetworkAdapter -VMHost "MyESXHost.mydomain.com" -
PortGroup vmkernel -VirtualSwitch $NewSwitch -IP
"192.168.0.10" -SubnetMask "255.255.255.0" -VMotionEnabled
$true
```

Configuring e-mail alerts

To use e-mail alerts, you must have vCenter. Two items need to be configured:

- Configure the SMTP and email addressing information in your vCenter server.

- Configure the alert to send an e-mail alert.

To configure the vCenter server, connect using the Virtual Infrastructure Client. Connect to your vCenter server and select from the Menu Bar Administration→ vCenter Server Settings → Mail. In this window you will identify the SMTP gateway that will send/relay the message either by DNS name or IP address and the email address of the sender of the address.

We have done this with Exchange, and there are a couple of items to note. First, the easiest way to do this is to configure your Exchange server's SMTP server to relay messages for the vCenter server's host IP. This can be done in the properties of the SMTP server on the Exchange server being targeted.

Second… this can generate a LOT of e-mail. If you set these thresholds too low, you need to make sure to set up the frequency and range settings in the alarm. The idea is to keep vCenter from sending 20 emails over a 10-minute period for the same problem just because of a little movement in the counter.

While you are connected to your vCenter server, select the host or virtual machine you want to create the e-mail alert for. Select the alarm tab for either a host or virtual machine. Change to the Definitions view. From this view you can create a new alarm and define an action that will send an e-mail notification to the defined e-mail address.

You will see some default alarms in there, but these cannot be modified.

Configuring SNMP

To use e-mail alerts in 4.0 you must have vCenter. Once vCenter is up and running, you need to configure two items:

- The SNMP Receiver information in your vCenter server

- The alerts to send an SNMP Trap.

To configure the vCenter server, connect using the Virtual Infrastructure Client. Connect to your vCenter server and select from the **Menu Bar Administration→ vCenter Server Settings→ SNMP**.

In this window you will identify the SNMP Receiver, either by DNS name or IP address that will receive the trap, the port that is to be used, and the community string. You can configure three additional trap receivers on this page as well.

While still connected to your vCenter server, select the host or virtual machine you want to create a specific alert for. Select the alarm tab for either a host or virtual machine. Change to the Definitions view by clicking on the definitions button. From this view you can create a new alarm and define an action that will send an SNMP notification to the defined SNMP Trap receiver(s).

Create a DRS or HA cluster

VMware added several of new features around Clusters with the release of vSphere. New additions include VM monitoring for HA, EVC mode and updates for power management and HA options.

Clusters can be created at a datacenter or folder within a datacenter within vCenter. You can create a new cluster by using the VI toolbar, right-clicking on a datacenter or folder and selecting 'New Cluster...' or by using the <Ctrl+l> shortcut.

When creating a new cluster you will be given the opportunity to configure VMware's DRS, HA and a few other features if you have the appropriate licenses. You may always configure these options at a later time.

To create a cluster:

1. Right Click a Datacenter and choose New Cluster (CTRL+L)

2. Name the cluster and select the feature(s) you with to configure.

3. Set VMware DRS automation level.

    a. Optionally, you can also configure Power Management if licensed.

4. Set the number of host failures your cluster will support, as well as the admission control setting that best fits your VMware HA policy.

    a. Optionally, you can set advanced options for VM settings and monitoring

5. Set VMware EVC Mode.

6. Configure the default location for VM swap files.

7. Once a cluster is configured with an ESX host and virtual machines, you may manage additional DRS and HA settings by editing the cluster's configuration.

DRS settings:

Rules – DRS allows the creation of virtual machine-based rules that enable you to isolate or keep VMs running on the same ESX host.

Virtual machine options – DRS also allows you to override the default DRS settings on a virtual machine basis. Each VM can be configured with its own unique automation level.

Power Management - DRS allows you to shutdown or suspend hosts automatically when the resource utilization falls below certain thresholds globally or on a per host basis.

VMware EVC:

VMware EVC ensures that all of the CPU resources are leveraging the same instruction sets to maximize VMotion compatibility.

HA settings:

For each virtual machine configured in the cluster, you may set a Restart Priority and Isolation Response individually.

New to vSphere is the ability to monitor within the Guest OS now for the VM heartbeat. If it detects the heartbeat is not alive, it can automatically reboot or restart the VM.

PowerCLI Example

The following shows how PowerCLI can be used to add new clusters with both DRS and HA settings:

```
Cmdlets
New-Cluster

Related Cmdlets
Get-Cluster
Move-Cluster
Remove-Cluster
Set-Cluster
EXAMPLE 1:
Adds a new cluster to the "Production" Datacenter with DRS
Enabled and set to FullyAutomated:

$DataCenter = Get-Datacenter "Production"

New-Cluster -Location $DataCenter -Name Accounts -DRSEnabled -
DRSMode FullyAutomated

EXAMPLE 2:
Adds a new cluster to the "Production" Datacenter with HA
Enabled and set to Failover for 1 host:

$DataCenter = Get-Datacenter "Production"

New-Cluster -Location $DataCenter -Name Accounts -HAEnabled -
HAFailoverLevel 1
```

Configuring Fault Tolerance

New to vSphere is Fault Tolerance, FT for short. FT brings the concept, first introduced in VMware Workstation, called Record – Replay to ESX. Unlike traditional HA or clustering with Active/Passive, FT mirrors everything from a primary VM to a secondary (failover) VM. In the event of a disruption on the primary host, the secondary VM takes over (with virtually no downtime). Essentially, the secondary VM is a mirror copy of the primary, including processing, memory and disk activities.

These steps assume you have configured the cluster for HA.

From vCenter:

1. Right click the VM you wish to protect, and click Fault
   Tolerance → Turn On Fault Tolerance

2. A message box will alert you that it will convert thin disks to
   thick, turn off DRS for the VM and set a memory
   reservation. Click Yes to turn on.

3. Once clicked, vCenter will create another VM and place it
   on another ESX host in the cluster. Once this is done you
   can see the status in the vSphere Client.

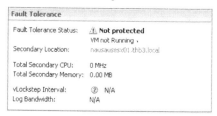

If everything is configured properly, the status will change to
"Protected" and you will be able to see the resources being used for FT.
Generally speaking, the resource load will be low for most FT VMs,
because the secondary is not doing processes such as downloading files
or serving client requests.

 **Because FT relies on new functionality in modern
processors, you must be running current generation
CPUs for FT to work.
FT uses HA & VMotion features, you will need to
ensure all of the HA/VMotion requirements are met
before FT can work.**

How do I configure sysprep?

In order for certain functionality in the vCenter 4.0 to work, VMware
requires that the Microsoft sysprep files be available and in a certain
location on the vCenter server.

You can download the sysprep files from Microsoft at the following
location:

www.microsoft.com/windows2000/downloads/tools/sysprep/default.a
sp.

Extract Q257813_w2k_spl_x86_en.exe to:

C:\Documents and Settings\All Users\Application
Data\VMware\VMware VirtualCenter\sysprep\1.1

If you extract the files to the 1.1 directory, sysprep will work with 2000, XP, and Server 2003, but we recommend that you use the specific version of sysprep for each version of the Windows OS.

To use the OS-specific versions of sysprep, copy the DEPLOY.CAB file from the \Support\Tools directory on the installation media and extract the files to the appropriate location listed below:

- Windows 2000: C:\Documents and Settings\All Users\Application Data\VMware\VMware VirtualCenter \sysprep\2k

- Windows XP: C:\Documents and Settings\All Users\Application Data\VMware\VMware VirtualCenter \sysprep\xp

- Windows XP x86_64: C:\Documents and Settings\All Users\Application Data\VMware\VMware VirtualCenter \sysprep\xp-64

- Windows 2003: C:\Documents and Settings\All Users\Application Data\VMware\VMware VirtualCenter \sysprep\srv2003

- Windows 2003 x86_64: C:\Documents and Settings\All Users\Application Data\VMware\VMware VirtualCenter \sysprep\srv2003-64

Deploying a VM from a template

These steps assume you have a template already created in vCenter.

From vCenter:

1. Choose the template you want to deploy from. If you do not see the templates in your inventory view, change the view by using the 'View' pull-down menu and selecting Inventory – VMs and Templates. (CTRL+SHIFT+V)

2. Right-click on the template to be deployed and choose "Deploy Virtual Machine from this Template." The Deploy Template wizard starts.

3. Name the new virtual machine.

4. Choose the host to place the virtual machine on (or cluster, depending on vCenter configuration).

5. Choose a resource pool, if you are using them.

6. Choose the datastore to use (all available VMFS volumes will be presented, so make sure to make your choice not only based on size but by the expected disk IO and throughput).

7. Choose a disk format (Same as the template, thin or thick).

8. Choose an option for the guest customization (to either customize or not). Customizing uses VMware automation to apply unique settings to the VM.

9. Choose if you want to power on the VM, and select Finish.

In vCenter 4.0, you can create and manage multiple datacenters. However, you cannot cross-deploy templates between datacenters. This means that you will have to export a template from one datacenter and re-import it into another. Another known Microsoft issue when deploying from a template is to have the Telephony service enabled or set to manual. Do not set the Telephony to disabled, as this will cause sysprep to fail. This is a Microsoft issue and is documented in KB836426. There have been reported issues that virtual machines cannot be deployed at all. If this is the case for you, you will need to reinstall vCenter. When reinstalling vCenter, do not overwrite the database.

PowerCLI Example

The following shows how PowerCLI can be used deploy new virtual machines from templates:

```
Cmdlets
New-VM
New-Template

Related Cmdlets
Get-VM
Move-VM
Remove-VM
Set-VM
Start-VM
Stop-VM
Suspend-VM
Get-Template
Remove-Template
Set-Template
EXAMPLE 1:
Deploys a virtual machine called NewVM from a template called
Windows2003SP1-GOLD to a host called MyESXHost.mydomain.com:

New-VM -Name "NewVM" -Template "Windows2003SP1-GOLD" -VMHost
(Get-VMHost "MyESXHost.mydomain.com"
```

EXAMPLE 2:
Creates a new template called Windows2003SP1-GOLD from an existing VM called TemplateVM and places it in the Production datacenter:

```
New-Template -VM (Get-VM "TemplateVM") -Name "Windows2003SP1-
GOLD" -Location (Get-Datacenter "Production")
```

Updating templates

If you want to apply Microsoft updates, other OS changes, new antivirus signatures, new backup agents, software updates, and VMware tools updates to your templates, it is now easier in vCenter 4.0. The process involves taking the template and converting it back to a virtual machine, and then back again. The process in vCenter 4.0 is now down to three steps vs. seven in vCenter 2.5.

1. Right-click on the template you are going to update.

2. Choose to "Convert to Virtual Machine" A Convert Template to Virtual Machine window displays.

3. Choose a host or cluster to place the VM on.

4. Choose a resource pool, if you are using them, and select Finish.

5. The template is now a VM.

You are now able to update you virtual machine with the required changes. When you are finished, you can right-click the virtual machine and convert it back to a template. We would suggest that you make this a new template and leave the existing template in place as a rollback point.

Creating a vCenter-based snapshot

vCenter-based snapshots are most often used for testing changes to VMs and reverting to the original state quickly. Snapshots have many uses, but this is one of the most common.

From vCenter:

1. Choose the VM you wish to take a snapshot of from the inventory.

2. Right-click on the virtual machine and choose "snapshot" The snapshot wizard starts.

3. Name your snapshot.

4. You can give a description of the snapshot.

5. Un-Select "Snapshot the virtual machine's memory"

6. Select "Quiesce guest file system (Needs VMware Tools installed)"

7. Select OK. A message box will display the progress of the snapshot and when it finishes.

To revert to the parent snapshot, you would:

1. Right-click the virtual machine.

2. Select Revert to snapshot.

You can also use the Snapshot Manager to select a previous snapshot other than your parent snapshot if you have multiple snapshots.

1. Right-click on the virtual machine.

2. Select snapshot.

3. Select Snapshot Manager.

4. Click the Go to button and select the snapshot you want to use.

Now for some gotchas surrounding snapshots:

Use them sparingly! If one virtual machine has too many snapshots, it can cause vCenter to have issues between the vCenter database and the ESX host. The virtual machine may not start, and vCenter can crash. If this happens, you will need to unregister the virtual machine from the COS. The syntax is `vmware-cmd -s unregister /path/to/the/.vmx`.

When un-selecting "Snapshot the virtual machine's memory", you prevent the system from downloading the entire contents of the VM's memory to disk. If the VM has an extremely large memory footprint(>16GB), this could cause the VM to be unavailable during the process.

Another known issue with snapshots is the comments field. Use the comments field sparingly, as there is a limit to how many characters can be entered. The limit is around 1024.

PowerCLI Example

The following examples show how PowerCLI can be used to manage all aspects of snapshots:

Cmdlets
```
Get-Snapshot
New-Snapshot
```

```
Remove-Snapshot
Get-VM
```

Related Cmdlets
```
Move-VM
Remove-VM
Set-VM
```
EXAMPLE 1:
Create a new snapshot on a VM Called PROD1:

```
New-Snapshot -Name "General Snapshot" -VM (Get-VM "PROD1")
```

EXAMPLE 2:
Create a new snapshot on all VMs:

```
New-Snapshot -Name "All Machine Snapshot taken today" -VM
(Get-VM)
```

EXAMPLE 3:
List snapshots for all VMs:

```
Get-VM | Get-Snapshot
```

EXAMPLE 4:
List all snapshots over 14 days old:

```
Get-VM | Get-Snapshot | Where { $_.Created -lt (Get-
Date).AddDays(-14)}
```

EXAMPLE 5:
Revert the VM called PROD1 to a snapshot which is called
"First Snapshot":

```
$VM = Get-VM -Name "PROD1"
$SnapshotName = $VM | Get-Snapshot -Name "First Snapshot"
$SnapshotName | Where-Object { $_.name -like
$SnapshotName.name } | ForEach-Object { Set-VM $VM -snapshot
$SnapshotName }
```

EXAMPLE 6:
Remove all snapshots on the VM called PROD1:

```
Get-VM "PROD1" | Remove-Snapshot -confirm:$False
```

Deleting/Cleaning up vCenter logs

The vCenter logs are stored as text files located in the file system of the
vCenter server. By default, they are located at C:\Documents &
Settings\All Users\Application Data\VMware\VMware Virtual
Center\Logs. Since the most recent log file is in use when the vCenter
server service is running, it must be stopped temporarily if you are to
clean them out.

1. Stop the "VMware vCenter Server" service.

2. Navigate to C:\Documents & Settings\All
    Users\Application Data\VMware\VMware Virtual
    Center\Logs.

3. Consider saving an archive copy of the log files. Select the vpxd-*.log files and send to "Compressed Folder." Rename the .zip file to something meaningful (include the current date as part of the filename). Move the .zip file to a safe location.

4. Delete the contents of C:\Documents & Settings\All Users\Application Data\VMware\VMware Virtual Center\Logs, including the vpxd-index file.

5. Restart the "VMware vCenter Server" service.

6. Verify that the vpxd-*.log file and the first log (vpxd-0.log) have been created.

Stopping the vCenter Server service will not affect the availability of any guest servers. However, any existing vSphere Client connections will be reset.
Also, all logs are automatically compressed using Tar + Gzip and rolls through a default of 9 historical copies plus the current log.

Recovering the vCenter server

Ensure that all connections to the vCenter database are stopped. You can view connections by connecting to the MS SQL Server with Enterprise Manager.

1. Depending on what type of database you're using, or if you have lost the DB also, restore it if needed.

2. Build a new vCenter server (new Windows build), or restore from backup.

3. Install/Re-install vCenter on your restored server.

4. Use the same settings that you had previously used to set up vCenter, specifically the IP address.

5. After setting up your ODBC connection, you'll be prompted to overwrite the existing data. Select No.

6. Continue through to the end of the installation.

Your vCenter server should be backed up and running with all of your configurations.

These steps are really there to place focus on selecting NO to the overwrite question. vCenter is a three-tier application with the vCenter server communicating with the database. In some organizations the database is located on the same server as the vCenter server. In these cases you may need to restore the host first (possibly along with the DB), then just validate connectivity and the state of the DB. If the DB is on a separate server, then the vCenter server is just a middle man and re-installing the app (even on a newly built server) and pointing it back to the existing database will work.

 The simplest approach in a small environment could be to have your vCenter as a VM. All you have to do is snap, store and restore.

Setting up roles and permissions in vCenter

Using groups/roles to organize users in vCenter simplifies the administration of your virtual infrastructure. You can use groups to organize users who require the same level of access within vCenter, thereby minimizing the amount of administrative overhead.

Access in vCenter is defined by what are called roles. The trick here is to understand that the way vCenter roles are used is kind of counter-intuitive to the way you think it should work.

First, you should understand that permissions in vCenter are applied through these roles. Windows users and/or group accounts can be added to vCenter objects then a permission/role can be assigned. These permissions/roles inherit from parent objects to child objects.

Generally, when you think of roles you think that you create a role that has a pre-defined set of permissions and object access, then a group or user is added to the Role. In vCenter, a Role is really a set of permissions. Then on objects in the inventory you add a user or group to the object with a specific Role/Set of permissions. See? It's confusing. Basically, look at the roles in VC as a set of permissions that can be applied to any object. Then you will still configure an object (datacenter, folder, VM, host, etc.) with a user and its permissions to the object, only the permissions may be preconfigured as a role.

By default, vCenter provides three pre-defined roles and six sample roles.

- No Access
- Read Only
- Administrator

- Virtual Machine Power User (sample)

- Virtual Machine User (sample)

- Resource Pool Administrator (sample)

- VMware Consolidated Backup User (sample)

- Datastore Consumer (sample)

- Network Consumer (sample)

You can view the permissions that have been assigned to roles by selecting Roles from the Home Menu, right-clicking on the role in the details window and choosing Edit.

vCenter also provides the ability to edit, clone, rename and delete existing roles. This can all be performed from the Roles menu and by right-clicking on the appropriate role.

As far as assigning these rights, you can assign a group to a role on any object in the vCenter inventory, including any of the following:

- Datacenters

- Clusters

- Resource groups

- Hosts

- Virtual machines

- vApps

- Folders

Adding a group to an object in the vCenter inventory can be performed by:

1. Select the Inventory from the menu bar.

2. Right-click on the object that you wish to assign the group to.

3. Choose Add Permission

4. Select Add from the Users and Groups window box

5. Choose the domain you wish to select the group from. You can also add local groups from the vCenter server.

6. Select "Show Groups First" from the drop-down menu.

7. Highlight the group in the Name box and choose Add. You can select multiple groups if they are separated by a semicolon. Click OK.

8. In the Assigned Role box choose a role to associate with the new group. You can choose to propagate the new role assignment to all child objects of the object you set the permission on.

 Permission assignments in vCenter work in a similar way to Windows folder structure security. With that in mind, when assigning permissions to groups you may find it easier to add the group to the root level of the vCenter inventory with limited amount of access and set the appropriate permissions on the objects that group needs access to farther down in the hierarchy.

Setting up alarms in vCenter

By default, most alarms are created at the vCenter object level. While you can create alarms at the individual VM or Object level, it is always best to create them at the highest level possible to ensure coverage of the alarms. It's much easier to create one rule for a group of VMs vs. the same rule for each VM or folder.

To create an alarm in the vSphere Client:

1. Right click the object and select Alarm → Add Alarm (CTRL+M)

2. Give the alarm a name and description.

3. Select the Alarm Type (This would be for what objects you wish to alarm against).

4. Select the Triggers Tab and Add.

5. This will add a generic alarm that you can modify each of the fields for, including:

   • Trigger Type – What metric/detail should I look at?

   • Condition – True or False? Greater/Less than?

   • Warning – At what level is it a warning?

   • Condition Length – How long at the Warning level until I alarm?

   • Alert – At what level is it an alert?

   • Condition Length – How long at the Alert level until I alarm?

6. Click OK to set the alarm

In addition to those two tabs, there are also Reporting & Action Tabs. Reporting allows you to set the frequency of how often the alarm should fire, if it exists for a long period of time. Actions can be anything you define from sending an email, to powering off a VM or even running a command or script.

Hosts

This section of the guide focuses on the Host ESX server itself. Most of the tasks found in this section can be accomplished either via the command line in the Console OS or via the vCenter client connected directly to the ESX host server.

For those who aren't comfortable with the console, don't worry. We've included plenty of step-by-step instructions to walk you through anything that's close to being complicated.

What can I do with the vSphere Web Access?

The vSphere Web Access is a web-based method for accessing and managing virtual machines in ESX Server and vCenter Deployments. This eliminates the need for installing the vSphere Client for users that only need access to administer virtual machines. However, vSphere Web Access has been disabled by default for security reasons. If needed it can be enabled via the Service Console:

```
service vmware-webAccess start
```

This is just a temporary solution. When the host is rebooted vSphere Web Access is disabled again. If it needs to be persistently enabled you can modify the run level:

```
chkconfig -level 345 vmware-webAccess on
```

Communication between the vCenter Server and the vSphere Web Access client is over TCP Port 443. VMware has certified vSphere Web Access use with Microsoft Internet Explorer 6.0(or later) and Mozilla Firefox 2.0(or later) for Windows and Linux. Web Access allows users to:

- Use a browser to view hosts and virtual machine details.

- Perform power operations on virtual machines.

- Edit a virtual machine's configuration and hardware.

- Generate VMware Remote Console URLs that users can use to access their virtual machines.

- Interact with the guest operating systems that are running on the virtual machines.

- Access ESX hosts and vCenter Servers from Linux systems.

How many ESX hosts can I have per DRS/HA cluster?

The simple answer to this is 32. VMware stated that up to 32 hosts can be in any HA or DRS cluster (cluster being logical in vCenter and physical because these hosts are all zoned to the same VMFS volumes). But in some rare cases the real answer to this may be deeper in the system than what vCenter can do and may lie in the number of VMs you have, the size of the hosts, and even LUN sizes. Below are two examples of when the max is NOT 32:

Example 1:

Environment (HUGE environment):

- Quad-processor-based host with an average of 30 VMs per host, with four paths from each host to each LUN

- 600 total virtual machines targeted in the next 12-18 months

- LUNs are going to be hosted on DMX storage with LUN sizes of 136GB (the SAN guy just won't go any bigger)

- Average VM requiring 40GB of writable space split across two vmdk files.

In this case you are getting about 2.5 VMs per LUN. If you do the math, you will need about 24 quad-processor hosts to host these 600 VMs (600/30 per host), which is well under the 32 max. But with 2.5 VMs per LUN you are going to need 240 LUNs (600/2.5). This is getting very close to the 256 LUN limit for ESX and will not even allow you to install ESX at this point if the LUNs are already exposed to the server at installation time. And if it does install, it may require some extra post-installation steps.

On top of this, with four paths to each LUN you have a total of 960 paths from each server. With a max of 1024 paths, you have only 64 paths remaining, or 16 new LUNs.

While this environment is out of reach for most organizations, it is still possible and could be a nightmare. Imagine a server with 960 paths to storage behind it… too much.

Example 2:

Environment:

- Dual Quad-processor-based host with 64GB of memory and with an average of 80 VMs per host

- A total of 1280 VMs in the cluster running on 16 hosts

- High Availability is a requirement

Although 1280 VMs is the supported maximum for a DRS / HA cluster this specific example is an unsupported configuration. Currently (ESX 4.0) the maximum amount of VMs on a single host in a DRS / HA cluster larger than 8 hosts is 40. In this example the cluster size is 16 hosts, which means the total amount of VMs per host can't exceed 40.

So how many hosts can you have in a cluster using DRS and HA, where the max is 32 but where you also have to consider the storage ramifications and the configuration maximums. For more information on this, see the storage sections in this guide or the "Configuration Maximums for VMware vSphere 4.0" guide.

PowerCLI Example

The following shows how PowerCLI can be used to report on cluster information:

```
Cmdlets
Get-Cluster
Get-VMHost

Related Cmdlets
Move-Cluster
New-Cluster
Remove-Cluster
Set-ClusterRemove-VMHost
Move-VMHost
Set-VMHost
Add-VMHost

EXAMPLE 1:
Reports a list of each cluster name and the number of hosts
within the cluster:

Get-Cluster | Select Name, @{N="NumHosts";E={@(($_ | Get-
VMHost)).Count}} | Sort Name
```

Connecting to the Console OS remotely

The Console Operating System (COS) uses SSH for remote connections. By default it doesn't allow straight telnet as telnet is considered unsecured. Most admins use a free SSH client called PuTTy, which you can download from this site:

http://www.chiark.greenend.org.uk/~sgtatham/putty/download.html.

Or just google™ for "putty" you'll get there in about two seconds.

By default, you won't be able to connect to the host using the root account. This is not to torment you; it's a common best practice for Linux and Unix-based systems and has been introduced by default with ESX 3. Simply create a user on the system (you can do this from the server console or by using the vSphere Client connected directly to the server) and give this user console access.

Once you have connected as this new user you can then execute the 'su' command to elevate your privileges (just have your root password handy). We recommend setting up "sudo" which is described in the security chapter.

 By using su -, you'll get the privileges of root as well as the shell which includes the environment variable paths. Translated: you'll be able to type in something like esxcfg-nics without having to include the path to it.

However, it is possible to enable root access via SSH.

1. Edit the SSHd_config located in the director /etc/SSH/SSHd:
   ```
   vi /etc/SSH/SSHd_config
   ```

2. Find the following line:
   ```
   PermitRootLogin no
   ```

3. Replace it with the following:
   ```
   PermitRootLogin yes
   ```

4. Restart the SSH daemon:
   ```
   service SSHd restart
   ```

Finding a file in the console

For you Windows guys who aren't familiar with Linux file systems, get familiar with the following commands (for sure the whereis command).

whereis – This command will help you find a file quickly. Wildcards are supported.

> **Example:** whereis esxtop
>
> **Returns:** esxtop: /usr/bin/esxtop /usr/man/man1/esxtop.1
>
> whereis [file]

find – This one will also help you find files quickly.

> **Example:** find / -iname '*.iso'
>
> **Returns:**
>
> /usr/lib/vmware/isoimages/freebsd.iso
> /usr/lib/vmware/isoimages/linux.iso

```
/usr/lib/vmware/isoimages/netware.iso
/usr/lib/vmware/isoimages/solaris.iso
/usr/lib/vmware/isoimages/windows.iso

find [path] [expression] [pattern]
```

grep – Will find text and text strings within files. There are several search options available.

Example: `grep -li "failed" *.log`

Returns: `boot.log`

```
grep <options> "Search String" [filename]
grep <options> [-e pattern] [file]
grep <options> [-f file] [file]
```

Connecting to ESX 4.x with WinSCP or PuTTY

PuTTY and WinSCP are fantastic tools that can assist Windows administrators in managing their hosts. Since the release of ESX 3.0, SSH using the root account has been disabled by default and has caused some confusion and problems for admins.

For PuTTY, this doesn't pose an issue, as you can connect as a different user and then use sudo to run a command with the appropriate permissions.

WinSCP is another story. The utility doesn't have a su function, so when you connect, your session will be quite restrictive. A basic workaround, while maintaining security and staying within best practices, would be to:

- Create a user with console access

- Create a new folder in a datastore

- Following the below table, change the permissions on the folder by executing chmod 775 foldername.

Number	Permission	Text Display
0	None	--
1	Execute	--x
2	Write	-w-
3	Write, execute	-wr
4	Read	r--
5	Read, execute	r-x
6	Read, write	rw-
7	Read, write, execute	rwx

This will allow your user, which is a member of the xxx group by default, to write to the folder.

Using root for general administration is a very poor practice. Allowing **SSH** access as root is even worse. You should do some research prior to flipping **SSH** for root. It's a quick fix, but something that should be discouraged. Also, changing permissions to 777 is not a good practice.

How to connect to an ESX host and configure it

Once you've installed ESX, you'll need to connect to it and configure it. Unless you're an experienced ESX admin, you'll typically connect to your host using the vSphere Client that comes on the vCenter CD or it can be downloaded from your ESX server's web interface. If you do not have the vSphere Client already installed on your workstation, use an Internet browser to browse to your server's Web Interface at http://YourServerName/. On this page you will see a link to "Download the vSphere Client." Click this link and use the package being downloaded to install the complete vSphere Client.

Once installed, start the client and in the initial logon box enter in your logon information (generally the root account the first time a server is installed). If you've already added a DNS entry for your host, then use the name. Otherwise, just use the IP address.

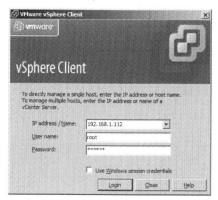

After you connect to your host, you'll notice that your window is divided in to two panes, with your host on the left. Highlight the host and then select the Configuration tab along the top of the right pane.

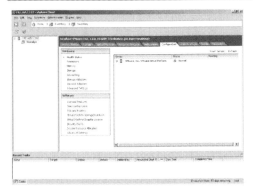

From this screen you'll be able to add virtual switches, scan for additional storage, format your VMFS, as well as numerous other tasks.

Now, if you're an advanced ESX administrator, you can connect to the Console Operating System through your favorite SSH client and then do most, if not all, of your configuration from the command line.

Adding the current path to your prompt

When you are troubleshooting your environment you will need to be absolutely certain you are running certain commands in the correct directory. By default the bash command prompt does not show the full path which can be confusing. You can use the "pwd" command to display the current path. Another option would be changing your prompt to reflect the current location. Use the command shown below as root or root equivalent:

```
mv /etc/bashrc /etc/bashrc.old
sed -e "s/\\h \\\W/\\h \\\w/g" /etc/bashrc.old > /etc/bashrc
```

Verifying/Configuring ESX post installation

Once you complete the installation of a basic ESX install, there are still a few items that you may wish to validate/configure on the ESX host in order to ready the host to support virtual machines in a production environment. While each environment is different we think the following list of items should be completed and will act as a good starting point for your base build:

The following assumes the ESX host is being managed by vCenter 4.x.

- Processors – verify ESX sees the correct number of processors in the vSphere Client. Configuration Tab – Processors link.

- Configure hyper-threading as needed by clicking the properties link, upper right hand corner of Processors page. (For Nehalem enable HT as there can be a substantial performance increase.)

- Memory – Set Service Console memory to the desired amount. Memory link, in Configuration tab – edit properties. For 4.0 we recommend the following:

  o   512MB for 20 or less VMs

  o   800MB for 20 or more VMs

  Memory is not as expensive as it used to be anymore thus 800MB might be preferable at all times. Did you notice that the default of 272MB for ESX 4.0 has been increased to 300MB for ESX 4.0?

  If any third-party tools or agents are running in the console set Service Console memory to 800MB.

- Storage link – Verify the ESX server is seeing all HBAs installed, and scan for existing VMFS volumes and add/create new volumes as needed.

- Networking – Create vSwitched or Distributed vSwitches for the ESX host; verify network speed and duplex for all network adapters.

- Licensing – Configure the license for the ESX host.

- DNS & Routing – Configure the host's DNS setting and default routing.

- Install and configure hardware monitoring agents for your ESX hardware.

- Configure SNMP on the ESX host (if needed).

- Configure NTP (time service).

- Create local users on ESX host, configure PAM if necessary.

PowerCLI Example

Many of the above tasks can be completed through PowerCLI, the below are a few examples of how to complete this:

Cmdlets
```
Get-VMHost
```

```
Get-View
Get-Cluster
```

Related Cmdlets
```
Move-Cluster
New-Cluster
Remove-Cluster
Set-ClusterRemove-VMHost
Move-VMHost
Set-VMHost
Add-VMHost
Get-VIObjectByVIView
```

EXAMPLE 1:
The following shows how PowerCLI can be used to detail host information:

```
$Information = @()
Foreach ($ESXHost in (Get-VMHost | Get-View | Sort-Object
Name)){
        $MyDetails = "" | Select-Object Name, Type, CPU, MEM
        $MyDetails.Name = $ESXHost.Name
        $MyDetails.Type =
$ESXHost.Hardware.SystemInfo.Vendor+ " " +
$ESXHost.Hardware.SystemInfo.Model
        $MyDetails.CPU = "PROC:" +
$ESXHost.Hardware.CpuInfo.NumCpuPackages + " CORES:" +
$ESXHost.Hardware.CpuInfo.NumCpuCores + " MHZ: " +
[math]::round($ESXHost.Hardware.CpuInfo.Hz / 1000000, 0)
        $MyDetails.MEM = "" +
[math]::round($ESXHost.Hardware.MemorySize / 1GB, 0) + " GB"
        $Information += $MyDetails
}
$Information
```

EXAMPLE 2:
The following shows how PowerCLI can be used to change the Service Console memory for all hosts to 800MB:

```
$ConsoleMemMB = 800
Get-VMHost | Get-View | %{(Get-View -Id
$_.ConfigManager.MemoryManager).ReconfigureServiceConsoleReser
vation($ConsoleMemMB*1MB)}
```

EXAMPLE 3:
The following shows how PowerCLI can be used to scan hosts in your infrastructure for new storage volumes:

For a Specific Host:
```
Get-VMHost "MyESXHost.mydomain.com" | Get-VMHostStorage -
RescanAllHBA
```

For a Specific Cluster:
```
Get-Cluster -name "MY CLUSTER" | Get-VMHost | Get-
VMHostStorage -RescanAllHBA
```

All Hosts in VC:
```
Get-VMHost | Get-VMHostStorage -RescanAllHBA
```

EXAMPLE 4:
The following shows how PowerCLI can be used to report the speed of each NIC for all hosts in your virtual infrastructure:

```
$Information = @()
Foreach ($VMHost in Get-VMHost | Get-View | Sort Name)
{
          $MyDetails = "" | select VMHost
          $MyDetails.VMHost = $VMHost.Name
          $pnic = 0
          Do
          {
                    $MyDetails | Add-Member -name "Nic$pnic" -
memberType NoteProperty -value
"$($VMHost.Config.Network.Pnic[$pnic].LinkSpeed.SpeedMb)MB"
                    $pnic ++
          }
          Until ($pnic -eq
($VMHost.Config.Network.Pnic.Length))
          $Information += $MyDetails
}
```

Configuring Consolidated Backup (VCB)

Of course before you start, you'll need to set up your environment.
Although this process is straightforward, it's highly advisable that you
read the VMware Consolidated Backup Documentation page for the
detailed requirements.

1. Build your VCB proxy.

   a. Build a Windows 2003 or Windows 2008
   physical machine with a NIC and an HBA. Do
   not connect it to the fabric yet.

   b. Install your third-party backup agent software,
   like Veritas.

   c. Disable automatic drive letter assignments by
   opening a command prompt and typing in:

   ```
   C:\>Diskpart <enter>
   DISKPART>automount disable <enter>
   DISKPART>automount scrub <enter>
   DISKPART>exit
   ```

2. Reboot, attach VCB Proxy to the SAN and configure/zone
   it to see the same fabric as your ESX hosts.

3. Install the Consolidated Backup Framework.

Using vcbMounter

vcbMounter is used to back up an entire virtual machine in the Service
Console. It creates a quiesced snapshot of the virtual machine. Before

you use it though, you'll need to set up **backuptools.conf** in
/etc/vmware.

Open it with a compliant editor and add the following:

```
VCHOST= vCenter Server that manages this ESX Host
USERNAME= vCenter user that has privileges to create or
register VM
PASSWORD= Password of the VC user
```

From the COS, type in the following:

```
vcbMounter -a ipaddr:X.X.X.X -r /destination
```

How do use vcbSnapAll

For a group of virtual machines, use **vcbSnapAll** instead of
vcbMounter.

```
vcbSnapAll -a ipaddr:X.X.X.X -r /destination
```

The great thing about theses command line utilities is that you're not
required to have VCB set up and can run it directly from the Service
Console.

How to remove a VMware Data Recovery snapshot

VMware Data Recovery (DR is a backup appliance which utilizes
snapshots, as VMware VCB also does, to quiesce the virtual machine.
Something we have all experienced is VMware VCB initiated snapshots
that have not been removed correctly. This issue can also occur when
using VMware DR. The difference is that this snapshot can't be
removed without changes to the descriptor files.

1. First identify the descriptors that need to be corrected.
   ```
   grep -I ddb.dele *-000???.vmdk
   ```

2. Replace ddb.deletable="false" with ddb.deletable="true" in
   all related files:
   ```
   for y in *-000???.vmdk; do sed 's/ddb.deletable =
   "false"/ddb.deletable = "true"/g' $y > temp; mv temp
   $y; done
   ```

3. Create a new snapshot via the vSphere Client or via the
   Service Console:
   ```
   vmware-cmd /vmfs/volume/vmname/vmname.vmx
   createsnapshot snap snap 0 0
   ```

4. Delete all snapshots:
   ```
   vmware-cmd /vmfs/volume/vmname/vmname.vmx
   removesnapshots
   ```

Configuring NTP

To enable your ESX host's clock to synchronize with the authoritative time source in your environment, the NTP daemon should be configured. To enable this, two files need to be modified and the NTP daemon has to be set to start automatically on server reboot.

The easiest approach is to configure this from the command line by echoing the settings into the files, rather than editing the files directly. Use the commands shown below as root or root equivalent:

```
echo "restrict 208.152.51.48 mask 255.255.254.0 nomodify
notrap noquery" >> /etc/ntp.conf
echo "server 208.152.51.48" >> /etc/ntp.conf
The following line should be added for redundancy
echo "208.152.51.48" >> /etc/ntp/step-tickers
```

Obviously you could just edit the files, but echoing these lines into the files is quick and painless. After doing this we would recommend you 'cat' the files to review your changes. This will show the contents of the files in the screen.

```
cat /etc/ntp.conf
```

Make sure the entries echoed into the file are correct.

The next step is to open the firewall on the server to allow NTP traffic:

```
esxcfg-firewall --enableService ntpClient
```

Set the NTP service to auto-start when the server is rebooted:

```
chkconfig --level 345 ntpd on
```

Restart the NTP daemon:

```
service ntpd restart
```

Check if time has been synchronized:

```
ntpdate -q 208.152.51.48
```

Synchronize your hardware clock to the system clock.

```
hwclock --systohc
```

If you're more the "GUI" type of guy you can configure it via the vSphere Client:

Note: The date and time values of the host have been translated into the local time of this vSphere Client.

PowerCLI Example

The below example shows how these tasks can be completed using PowerCLI:

Cmdlets
```
Add-VMHostNtpServer
Remove-VMHostNtpServer
Get-VmHostService
Start-VmHostService
Get-VmhostFirewallException
Set-VmhostFirewallException
```

Related Cmdlets
```
Stop-VMHostService
Restart-VMHostService
```

EXAMPLE 1:
The following shows how PowerCLI can be used to remove the default ntp server and add your own:

```
$VMHost = "MyESXHost.mydomain.com"
$NTPServer = "ntp.mydomain.com"
Remove-VMHostNtpServer -VMHost $VMHost -NtpServer
'127.127.1.0'
Add-VMHostNtpServer -VMHost $VMHost -NtpServer $NTPServer

Get-VmHostService -VMHost $VMHost | Where-Object {$_.key -eq
"ntpd"} | Start-VMHostService
Get-VmhostFirewallException -VMHost $VMHost -Name "NTP Client"
| Set-VMHostFirewallException -enabled:$true
```

Manually setting the date and time

To set the date and time on the ESX host, you'll have to connect to the Service Console using an SSH client or access the console directly or via iLO/DRAC card. In either case, you will need to login as root or elevate your privileges via su to root or use sudo. Once at the console, use the date command to set the time and date:

```
date -s yyyymmdd [return]
date -s hh:mm [return]
```

> **Note that you don't have to run BOTH commands, but if you set the date it will reset the clock to 00:00 and you will (more than likely) need to set the time again.**

We recommend setting up NTP on your ESX so you don't constantly have to monitor or set the time. Having a synchronized time eases troubleshooting when a time-line needs to be created as well as being a requirement for many many environments.

Changing the ESX host's time zone

Sometimes errors are made during install where the time zone is set improperly on the host. The fix for this is a simple but often misunderstood process for Windows admins not familiar with Linux.

The time zone in ESX, like more standard variants of Linux, is set through a symbolic link to **/etc/localtime**, which is a file in the **/usr/share/zoneinfo** directory. The link corresponds to the time zone that you're in. If you look in the directories under **/usr/share/zoneinfo** you can see what time zones are available.

To set the time zone you need to create the symbolic link to the proper country/city/time zone in the zone info directory using the 'ln' command

```
ln -sf /usr/share/zoneinfo/<country>/<city> /etc/localtime
```

So in my case, I would need to set this to Central time since we are located in Chicago. You should choose the proper time zone for your site. My command would look like:

```
ln -sf /usr/share/zoneinfo/US/Central /etc/localtime
```

Remember this is Linux and items are case-sensitive.

Also, you might as well verify the **clock** file in **/etc/sysconfig.** This sets whether the hardware clock is stored as UTC or GMT. In most cases it should be set to UTC=true.

Editing files on the host server

By far, the most common command line editor available to any *nix device is vi. Although you can edit files in many different ways at the console of an ESX server, vi is readily available on any system (yes, it is available for Windows as well). In the ESX world 'nano' is another program often used to edit files on the console. Nano is by far the quickest/easiest to learn and can be used by running nano then the file name you want to edit:

```
nano /root/myGreatFile.txt
```

vi works the same way:

```
vi /root/myGreatFile.txt
```

Nano will show you a list of available commands (to save, not save, exit, etc.) at the bottom of the editing screen. For anyone new to Linux/ESX we highly recommend you just use nano, but if you want to use vi, below is a quick primer.

Once vi has a file open, you can navigate the file using the arrow keys (or h, j, k, or l where h=left, j=down, k=up, and l=right) on the keyboard. To make actual edits to the file, a command needs to be given to vi. To exit any command, hit the esc key. The following table provides an overview of common vi commands.

vi Command	Purpose
i	Start inserting text at the cursor's position.
I	Start inserting at the start of a line
a	Appends at the current cursor position
A	Appends at the end of the line
o (lower case "oh")	Starts a new line at the below cursor's position
O (upper case "Oh")	Starts a new line above the cursor's position
0 (zero)	Moves the cursor to the beginning of the line.
/	Starts a search – enter what you are looking for and select Enter.
n	Finds the next occurrence of what you are looking for.
N	Find the occurrence of what you are looking for in reverse
dd	Deletes the current line
dw	Deletes the current word starting at the cursor's position
D	Deletes from the cursor's position to the end of the line.

vi Command	Purpose
yy	Cuts the current line
p	Puts the yanked line at the cursor's position
u	Un-does the current change made
ZZ	Write and quit vi

Many commands require the colon ":" to be pre-pended to the command so it can be executed. These commands interact directly with vi:

vi Command	Purpose
:help	Enters vi's help system
:q	Quit vi
:q!	Quit vi and ignore changes
:w	Write changes
:wq	Writes and quits vi
:wq!	Forces a write of the file and then forces vi to quit

Using the above commands, you should be able to make simple changes to files using vi.

Copying files between hosts

Secure File Transfer (scp) from the console is an easy way to copy files between hosts. Before you use it, you'll need to enable the firewall to allow SSH client access. That can be done from the vSphere Client, Configuration tab, or from the console by typing in:

```
esxcfg-firewall -e SSHClient
```

Examples

To use SCP, your syntax is 'SCP sourcefile targetfile'. The thing that slows most people down is copying files from or to a remote host and getting that into the syntax. When designating a remote file use user@hostname:/path/filename. This can be used as either the source or target. Your local file (whether source or target) can simply be referenced by its local path by excluding everything prior to an including the ':'.

To copy a file from your local host to remote one:

```
scp /path/myfile userid@hostname:/path/myfile
```

Copying from a host to your local one:

```
scp userid@hostname:/path/myfile /path/myfile
```

You can also use scp to copy files to and from a Windows host, provided you've installed OpenSSH. This gives the same functionality from the command line.

Copy a vmdk from a Windows host running OpenSSH to a local ESX host.

```
scp user@host:c:/share/myfile /path/filename
```

 If your file or directory has a space in it, you can either fill it with \ or *(asterisk) or ? for a single character space. Single and double quotes do not work.

Using the CD-ROM/floppy on the host

On many Linux-based systems (which the Console OS is), when a CD-ROM or floppy disk is placed in the server, it is not readily accessible (mounted). There is an additional step that must be done to use the disk. To be able to access a CD-ROM or floppy drive in the Console OS, follow these steps:

1. Place a CD in the CD-ROM (and close the door) or insert a floppy disk into the floppy disk drive.

2. Log into the Console OS as root.

3. At the prompt:

   To access the CD in the CD-ROM drive, type:

   ```
   mount /mnt/cdrom
   ```
   To access a floppy disk type

   ```
   mount /mnt/floppy
   ```

4. To access the data, use the cd command and change directories to either /mnt/cdrom or /mnt/floppy

5. When you no longer need to use the CD in the CD-ROM drive or the floppy disk, you must un-mount the media. At the prompt type to un-mount your media:

   ```
   umount /mnt/cdrom
   umount /mnt/floppy
   ```

6. You can now eject the media.

On many systems, if you do not un-mount the CD-ROM, you will not be able to eject the CD from the CD-ROM drive, which we think is very cool and funny to watch sometimes... Before making a service call for a bad CD-ROM drive (which is also funny to watch), login as root and un-mount the CD-ROM.

Creating a CD-based ISO

With ESX, accessing a floppy disk or CD is painfully slow. Using an image increases the reading of the media in a virtual machine to a point where (at times) it is quicker to take an image before attempting to use the media. Also, you may want to store common floppy or CD images somewhere to use them remotely without having to put a disk in a physical drive (it is a virtual world, right?).

To create an ISO from a physical CD-ROM in an ESX host, first mount the CD from the Service Console:

1. Place a CD in the CD-ROM

    Log into the Console OS as root. To access the CD in the CD-ROM drive, type:

    ```
    mount /mnt/cdrom
    ```

2. Use the 'dd' command to create the ISO (note the path below assumes the target file is /vmimages/mycdrom.iso):

    ```
    dd if=/dev/cdrom of=/vmimages/mycdrom.iso bs=32k
    ```

    You can then mount this ISO image as a CD within a VM. You could also copy the ISO to a shared volume so VMs from multiple hosts could use it. When you no longer need to use the CD in the CD-ROM drive or the floppy disk, you must un-mount the media. At the prompt type either to un-mount your media: `umount /mnt/cdrom`.

    You can now eject the media.

The ISO image can now be used as a CD-ROM device for a virtual machine. If this is a bootable CD-ROM, the VM would even boot from it if the CD is connected at power-on.

 The bs and count arguments of the dd command are needed when making images of floppy disks.

> bs – Means read and write **512** bytes at a time
> count – The number of blocks to copy.

Creating a floppy image (FLP)

To create an FLP image of a physical floppy, from the Service Console insert the floppy you wish to use as a base, then mount the floppy:

Insert a floppy disk into the floppy disk drive.

Step 1: Log into the Console OS as root.

At the prompt:

To access a floppy disk, type

```
mount /mnt/floppy
```

Step 2: Like the CD, use 'dd' to create the flp image:

```
dd if=/dev/fd0 of=/vmimages/floppyfile.flp bs=512
count=2880
```

When you no longer need to use the floppy disk, you must un-mount the media. At the prompt, type to un-mount your media:

```
umount /mnt/floppy
```

You can now eject the media.

> **Note:** "dd" does not use error checking. You may want to use CD writing software for making ISOs that will be used for things like OS installs.

Can't we just use Windows to create the FLP image?

Another way to make a floppy image is to use a program called Winimage. You can use Winimage to create a floppy image file on a Windows machine. When you create the file, save it as a file type of IMA (a floppy image file). Once saved you can rename the file extension to .FLP and use that instead of a file created using the 'dd' command. The FLP file you create on Windows can be copied using something like WinSCP to VMFS volume on a host and used just like any other FLP file.

Using FLP and ISO images from the console

If you have images of CD or floppy diskettes (ISOs or FLPs) on the ESX server, it is possible to mount those images to view them in the Console OS.

To mount an ISO of a CD-ROM where /vmimages/myCD.iso is the ISO:

```
mount -o loop -t iso9660 /vmimages/myCD.iso /mnt/cdrom
```

Use the umount command to un-mount the ISO image.

To mount an image of a floppy diskette:

```
losetup /dev/loop0 /vmimages/someFloppy.flp
mount /dev/loop0 /mnt/floppy
```

To un-mount the floppy image, follow these steps:

```
umount /mnt/floppy
losetup -d /dev/loop0
```

One final note on using images – the images created with dd do not contain any validation during creation. If you require a higher quality image of media, you should use commercial software.

Changing an ESX server name

Renaming your host is actually a simple process but requires a few steps:

1. In the vSphere Client either power down or migrate all of the VMs to another ESX host.

2. Put the host in Maintenance mode.

3. If this host is managed by a vCenter server, remove it from VC.

4. Connect directly to the host using the vSphere Client.

5. On the Configuration tab, select DNS and Routing and then Properties.

6. Rename the host and reboot.

7. Add the host back to VC.

8. Power up or migrate the virtual machines back to the host.

Changing a host's IP address

Changing the IP of your ESX server (i.e., the IP address of the Service Console for your host) can be done a couple of different ways. The simplest way for new admins is using the vSphere Client.

The process of changing the IP involves creating a temporary Service Console, moving the IP, then removing the temporary console connection:

1. In the vSphere Client, select the host on which you want to change the IP.

2. Find the configuration tab on the right side of the vSphere Client.

3. Select the Networking link from the Configuration tab.

4. Select the properties of your Service Console connection.

5. Click the Add button under the Ports tab.

6. Create a temporary Service Console, but use a different name like Service Console 1.

7. Enter a different IP address along with a subnet mask and default gateway.

8. Now, select the original Service Console connection, click Edit and change the IP address. Your vSphere Client will disconnect.

9. Reconnect using the new IP address.

10. Delete the temporary Service Console.

You can also change the IP address from the command line if you feel comfortable with it. For this we recommend using an iLO or DRAC type connection to the server or actually be standing at the server's console when this is done. Use the esxcfg-vswif command to change the IP:

```
esxcfg-vswif -i <ip> <vswif>
```

In this example we want to change the Service Console's IP to 10.11.1.198:

```
esxcfg-vswif -i 10.11.1.198 vswif0
```

If you also needed to change the subnet mask at the same time, you could add the '-n' switch to the command:

```
esxcfg-vswif -i 10.11.1.198 -n 255.255.255.0 vswif0
```

Finally, once you have made the change, restart the service by executing:

```
service mgmt-vmware restart
```

Regenerating a server certificate

If you have just been in the section about renaming a host you may have figured out that your server cert now no longer matches your server name. In this case you need to regenerate your server certificate.

From page 171 of the ESX Configuration Guide; you can generate new certificates for your ESX host by:

1. Change directories to /etc/vmware/ssl

2. Create backups of any existing certificates by executing the following commands:

    ```
    mv rui.crt orig.rui.crt
    mv rui.key orig.rui.key
    ```

3. Enter the following command to restart the vmware-hostd process:

    ```
    service mgmt-vmware restart
    ```

4. Confirm that the ESX Server host generated new certificates by executing the following command comparing the time stamps of the new certificate files with orig.rui.crt and orig.rui.key:

    ```
    ls -lha .
    ```

Checking ESX host log files

There are two methods for checking your host's log files in vSphere 4.0. You can use the vSphere Client (vSphere Client) or the Console OS.

To use the GUI method: use the vSphere Client connected to your ESX host, click on the Admin button on the navigation bar and select the log you wish to check.

To use the Console OS you will need to connect to your ESX host either from the physical console or via SSH using an SSH client such as PuTTy. Once in a console session, change to the directory where the logs are stored and type the following:

```
cd /var/log/
```

Below is a partial list of the most common logs that are written by the host and their location:

```
/var/log/vmware/hostd.log      ESX Server 4.x Service Log
/var/log/messages              Service Console Log
/var/log/vmkernel              VMkernel Messages
/var/log/vmkwarning            VMkernel Warnings
/var/log/vmware/vpx/           vSphere Client Agent log
/var/log/vmware/aam/           VMware HA Log files
```

 When using the COS you will need to log in as a user (most likely root) that has access to the /var/log/ directory

PowerCLI Example

The below example shows how PowerCLI can be used to display the log information:

Cmdlets
```
Get-VMHost
Get-LogType
Get-Log
```

Related Cmdlets
```
Remove-VMHost
Move-VMHost
Set-VMHost
Add-VMHost
```

EXAMPLE 1:
The following shows how to view the type of logs which can be viewed by PowerCLI:

```
Get-LogType -VMHost (Get-VMHost "MyESXHost.MyDomain.com")
```

EXAMPLE 2:
The below example shows how to retrieve the vmkernel log from "MyESXHost.MyDomain.com":

```
(Get-Log -VMHost (Get-VMHost "MyESXHost.MyDomain.com")
vmkernel).Entries
```

Upgrading from previous ESX versions

The process of upgrading your current ESX environment will be determined by your environment's configuration. With ESX you basically have two types of environments: ones managed by vCenter and those which are a collection of standalone ESX hosts.

The actual process for upgrading an ESX environment is broken down into four stages. These stages must be followed in order to achieve a successful upgrade. The following is an overview of the process for upgrading each type of environment.

vCenter environment

If your environment is managed by a vCenter server you will need to upgrade the vCenter server first. The following is the order that you must upgrade your ESX environment:

1. Upgrade your vCenter server including Update Manager, VI Client.

2. Upgrade your ESX hosts.

3. Upgrade your virtual machines (hardware).

4. Upgrade the VMware tools on your virtual machines.

Standalone environment

If your environment is a collection of standalone ESX hosts, your upgrade will consist of three stages. The following is the order that you must upgrade your ESX environment:

1. Upgrade your VI Client and the Host Update Utility.

2. Upgrade your ESX hosts.

3. Upgrade your virtual machines.

4. Upgrade the VMware tools on your virtual machines.

The following are the recommended steps to perform when upgrading a standalone ESX host:

Standalone ESX host upgrade

1. Verify that your ESX hardware is on the hardware compatibility list.

2. Commit any snapshots assigned to virtual machines and change their disks to persistent mode. This is not required but strongly recommended by VMware.

3. Disconnect any shared storage from the ESX host. This is not required but strongly recommended by VMware.

4. Start the Host Update Utility.

5. Add a host to the utility via "Host -> add host"

6. Type the location of the ESX installation file(iso) to use or browse to the location and select the iso file.

7. Accept the license agreement and select next.

8. Type the administrative account, a host compatibility check will now occur.

9. Select the datastore and size of the Service Console virtual disk. VMware recommends that you select a datastore that is local to the ESX host. The Service Console VMDK requires at least 8.4GB of available space. (Only /boot, vmkcore and the VMFS partition are physical partitions on the disk!)

10. Optional; Enable or disable automatic rollback. We recommend enabling it in case your hardware or one of the components is not compatible or causing issues.

11. Optional; Automate post-upgrade configuration by adding a script. We do not recommend a post upgrade configuration script. If post upgrade configuration is needed consider a fully automated rebuild

12. Optional; Select Roll back the upgrade if the post-upgrade script fails and select the number of seconds(0 to 180 seconds) for the installer to wait before it rolls back the upgrade if the post-upgrade script fails.

13. Next, Finish… Just wait for Host Update Utility to get the job done.

Clustered ESX host upgrade

1. Verify that your ESX hardware is on the hardware compatibility list.

2. Commit any snapshots assigned to virtual machines and change their disks to persistent mode. This is not required but strongly recommended by VMware.

3. Disconnect any shared storage from the ESX host. This is not required but strongly recommended by VMware.

4. Open the vSphere Client.

5. Make sure you have downloaded the latest updates.

6. Right click your host and select "scan for updates".

7. Select either "Upgrade".

8. Click "Scan".

9. When finished scanning right-click the host and select "remediate".

10. Select the baseline to apply to the chosen object(s).

11. Click next.

12. Agree with the terms and conditions and click next.

13. Pick a location for the Service Console VMDK.

14. Deselect any patches if needed.

15. Give the "schedule" a unique name.

16. Select immediately or schedule the remediation.

17. Click next

18. Review the chosen options and click finish

Datastore upgrade

Do I need to upgrade my datastore when upgrading from ESX 3.x to vSphere? No it is not necessary to upgrade in order to take advantage of the new features, it's even not possible to do a minor upgrade. The only way of running VMs on VMFS 3.33 is reformatting the LUN, this means migrating virtual machines with Storage VMotion first.

Reviewing host and guest performance/utilization

Viewing performance information from your hosts or guests is pretty simple. You can use either the vSphere Client connected to the vCenter server or connected right to the ESX server you wish to look at. Another option is to use command line (console) commands to view real-time performance/utilization. The vSphere Client also allows you to either view the graphs within the client or export a performance report to an Excel spreadsheet.

Within the vSphere Client you can view host performance by selecting the inventory view for "hosts and clusters" or use a hot keys "CTRL-SHIFT-H." Select the host or VM you wish to look at then select the Performance tab. This will default to a real-time chart showing CPU utilization for that object. If you wish to look at a different metric, just click the "Change chart options" link at the top of the graph.

If you want to export performance information into an Excel spreadsheet you can do this from the Performance tab by clicking on the export button (looks like a disk in the right-hand corner) or by right-clicking on the object in the inventory view and selecting "Report performance" from the menu. In either case the same window opens and allows you to select how far back you wish to look at the data for (hours, days, weeks, or months) and which specific metrics you wish to export.

From the console you can view real-time performance of the host or VMs by using a command called 'esxtop.' To get at this tool open a terminal session to your server and (using an account with permissions to do so or as 'root') run:

```
/usr/bin/esxtop
```

What you will see as output may look convoluted at first, but really it is just VMware's version of the Linux command 'top'. This will bring up a default esxtop window that will give you some basic stats for the CPU view. This includes things like the amount of uptime, the Physical CPU usage (PCPU), Logical CPU usage (LCPU) and individual VM/process information. You will also notice that each of the VMs is shown with its friendly name and not the VM world ID like in the previous version of ESX.

You can change views in esxtop to look at any of the core resources by simply tapping the key of the first letter for the resource, C for CPU (default view), D for Storage Adapter, M for memory, N for Network, U for Storage device and V for Storage virtual machine. You can also change the fields being viewed by hitting the 'f' key. In each of the different displays you will be shown a list of available fields that can be removed or added. With "o" you can change the order in which fields appear.

To save your configuration simply hold the Shift key while clicking 'W". This will write out the esxtop config for use the next time you load it.

To exit out, hold the "CTRL" key while clicking 'c' and esxtop will shut down.

For more information on esxtop
http://communities.vmware.com/docs/DOC-9279

Backing up an ESX host/configuration

There are many options to use when backing up ESX hosts. It would not be practical here to detail all of the installation procedures for various backup agents that are available. Instead, this section will discuss under what situation you should consider backing up an ESX host and what should be backed up if you do. How to install the agent will be up to you and the vendor.

One thing to consider when deciding whether or not to back up your hosts is the amount of effort you will spend restoring the host as opposed to just rebuilding it. When restoring a host from backup you will have to build the host, install the backup agent, and THEN restore the backup. This can be a time-consuming process. On the other hand, rebuilding an ESX server is a relatively simple process made even easier when using deployment tools such as Altiris Deployment Server, ESX Deployment Appliance or Ultimate Deployment Appliance.

When the host fails, the primary concern is to get the virtual machines that resided on that host up and running as soon as possible. Therefore, the main concern when considering backing up ESX hosts is the virtual machine files and not the host itself. Virtual machine files can be stored in two different locations.

Remote storage and SAN-connected hosts

When an ESX host maintains virtual machine files on remote storage (SAN, iSCSI or NFS) the need for installing a backup agent to back up the virtual machine files is greatly reduced.

When deciding to install backup agents to ESX hosts when using remote storage, there are two scenarios to consider: multiple host environments (clustered) and single SAN-connected hosts.

In the clustered environment in which multiple hosts have access to the same storage (and therefore the same virtual machines), a host failure no longer means extended downtime for the VMs when using vSphere 4 HA ability. Even registering the virtual machines to a new host in order to get them running is a fairly quick process. This provides some flexibility with respect to the time you have to get the failed host up and running.

In a situation in which a single host is using remote storage and the host failure results in extended downtime for your virtual machines, you will have to determine if restoring the failed host from backup will provide you with a method to get the virtual machines running sooner than simply rebuilding the host and registering the VMs. Depending on the configuration of your ESX host, this may indeed be the case.

Local storage host

Hosts using local storage to house virtual machines present a difficult situation. When these hosts fail there is no easy way to get the virtual machines up and running short of rebuilding the host. Once again we need to weigh the potential benefit of restoring from backup as opposed to rebuilding the host. The main concern here is which method will be quickest for your particular deployment of ESX.

What should be backed up

If you have decided to back up your ESX hosts, the files and directories you should concentrate on really depend on the configuration of your hosts. Remember that you will have to perform an installation of ESX using the original hostname and IP information, and then install the backup agent prior to restoring configuration files.

The following are examples (and should not be considered a complete list) of considerations for backup:

ESX configuration files – contents of the /etc/vmware directory, including esx.conf

Security files – local password files, group file, Kerberos files, etc.

Network files – hosts file, NTP file if used, etc.

Virtual machine files – If using local storage to house virtual machines, the contents of the virtual machine directories on the VMFS volumes, possibly excluding the VMDKs, then handling the VMDKs with snapshots.

Keep in mind that scripting a cron job can also be used as a backup strategy. You can grab the files needed, and then replicate these off of the ESX host to an NFS mount. Once the server is rebuilt you can then connect to the mount and copy the files back to the rebuilt host. However we prefer a scripted installation.

Another approach that some people on the VMTN Community forums have is scheduling a "vm-support" dump once a week. This dump file gets offloaded to a shared disk and can be used for restoring a host or troubleshooting purposes.

When installing backup agents on ESX host servers, you should account for the additional overhead on the COS by dedicating more memory to the Service Console.

Recovering a host

In every production (and in most cases development and test) virtual infrastructure, a recovery model of some type exists. Depending on the configuration of your environment, this may be achieved by using ESX host backup agents, imaging or bare metal installations. You can even use scripting to create cron jobs that back up the essential ESX host configuration files as a strategy. This section details steps that are needed to restore a failed host when using backup agents.

When ESX host backup agents are used to back up configuration files (and in some instances virtual machine files), a base ESX server installation is still needed in order to complete the restore. The reason for this is that the backup agent needs to be running on the server being restored. This base installation can be performed manually, by imaging or using a deployment tool such as Altiris Deployment Server. In each case you will have to follow certain steps during recovery.

SAN-connected hosts recovery

1. If the host was a member of a cluster, remove it from the cluster in vCenter.

2. Remove the host from the vCenter inventory.

3. Disconnect the failed ESX host from the SAN.

4. If the host failed due to hardware, replace the failed hardware.

5. Reinstall the ESX host using the same hostname and IP address.

6. Install backup agent software on host.

7. Restore configuration files from backup and reboot server when complete.

8. Verify the configuration of the host.

9. Reconnect the host to the SAN.

10. Add the host back to the vCenter inventory.

11. If the host was a member of a cluster, add the host back to the cluster. DRS will load balance the environment within a reasonable amount of time.

 A reboot will be required after replacing ESX host files for them to take affect.

Applying patches to the host

From time to time VMware releases patches or updates to their products. These patches might address a bug in the software, add new hardware support or address security issues. A readme text file usually accompanies the released patch describing the reason for the patch and applicable installation instructions.

The first thing that you should do when a patch is released is to determine if this patch addresses an issue in your environment or possibly a security issue with the product. You should categorize these patches as Critical or Non-Critical and then decide on the timeline for the application of the patch. VMware already categorizes the patches in three classifications; General, Critical and Security. We recommend installing at least Critical and Security, but preferably all.

After you have reviewed the patch information and have decided to implement the patch, you will need to develop an implementation process. The actual steps for implementing the patch will vary from environment to environment, but the overall process is the same. Listed below are overviews of the process for implementing a patch in an environment with or without vCenter.

vCenter managed environment

1. Review the knowledge base articles which are referred to in the patch download location or the update manager.

2. Download all patches via a scheduled task.

3. Right-click a host and select "Scan for Updates".

4. Select either "Patches" or "Upgrade".

5. Click "Scan".

6. When finished scanning right-click the host and select "remediate".

7. Select the baseline to apply to the chosen object(s).

8. Click next.

9. Agree with the terms and conditions and click next.

10. Review the selected patches and deselect any if needed.

11. Give the "schedule" a unique name.

12. Select immediately or schedule the remediation.

13. Click next

14. Review the chosen options and click finish

Note: If the patch requires it VMware Update Manager will automatically place the host in maintenance mode.

Standalone server environment

1. Review the knowledge base articles which are referred to in the patch download location or the update manager.

2. Verify that you have current backups of all virtual machines running on the ESX host.

3. Shut down all running virtual machines on the ESX host.

4. Open the Host Update Utility.

5. Download the latest patches by clicking "file" and "download patches from VMware".

6. Select the host or add a host and click "Scan for patches".

7. If patching is needed click "Upgrade".

8. Update the VMware tools on the virtual machines if applicable.

Setting COS memory allocations

Protecting or setting limits on the Service Console memory allocation should be done to ensure that the COS has the required memory resources that your environment requires. Requirements for the services console differ for each unique environment. Items like monitoring, backup or security agents contribute to the amount of memory the COS will need to function successfully.

The Service Console memory allocation is set at the ESX host level and needs to be configured individually for each ESX host in your environment. Making changes to an ESX host Service Console memory allocation can be done from within the vSphere Client.

To change an ESX host memory resource allocation, use the System Resources Allocation link from an ESX host configuration tab. In the System Resources Allocation window select the Advanced option. The advanced option button will open the System Resource Pools window. Navigate in the pools window until you find the 'console' option. Click on the 'console' option and the details windows will update with the current setting. To change the setting click on the Edit Settings link in the details window.

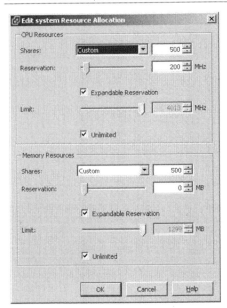

Edit the memory resources for the services console by selecting the appropriate amount of shares, reservation or limit your ESX host requires.

Note that it is also possible to give a specific feature or module a limit or reservation when you select "Advanced".

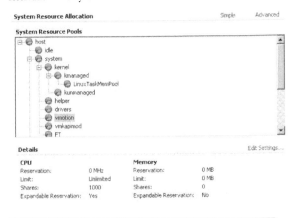

Shutting down an ESX server

We assume here that you have already powered off the virtual machines on this host or moved them to a new host via VMotion. The trick here is that while ESX can be set up to shut down your guest, it tends not to do a perfect job at it and/or it takes forever for your host to shut down while waiting on the VMs. Anyway, once you have taken care of the VMs (long story short don't let ESX handle their shutdown) then you can shut down the host in one of two ways:

From vCenter:

1. Select the host from inventory

2. Right-click on the host and select "maintenance mode"

3. All VMs will be VMotioned to other hosts

4. When all VMs have been VMotioned and maintenance mode has completed right-click on the host and select "shutdown"

You can also choose shutdown from the Summary commands tab.

From the COS:

1. Logon with root privileges

2. Put the Host into maintenance mode:
   ```
   vimsh -n -e /hostsvc/maintenance_mode_enter
   ```

3. Type 'shutdown'

PowerCLI Example

The following shows how PowerCLI can be used to put a host into maintenance mode and also shutdown multiple hosts:

```
Cmdlets
Get-Cluster
Get-VMHost

Related Cmdlets
Move-Cluster
New-Cluster
Remove-Cluster
Set-Cluster
Remove-VMHost
Move-VMHost
Set-VMHost
Add-VMHost

EXAMPLE 1:
```
The example below puts MyESXHost.mydomain.com into maintenance mode:

```
(Get-VMHost "MyESXHost.mydomain.com" | Get-
View).EnterMaintenanceMode_Task(-1, $true)
```

EXAMPLE 2:
Shutdown all ESX Hosts:

```
Get-VMHost | ForEach-Object {Get-View $_.ID} | ForEach-object
{$_.ShutdownHost_Task($TRUE)})
```

Licensing the ESX host

To license your installed ESX host, you'll need to connect to your host vCenter using the vSphere Client. After you have connected, highlight the host in the left pane. On the right side, select the Configuration tab.

There will be two boxes to the left of the pane: Hardware and Software. In the Software group, select "Licensed Features" and then edit.

As of vSphere 4.0 the license server has been deprecated. You can also centrally add a license to every single host by using the vCenter Licensing view to assign licenses. (Home -> Administration -> Licensing)

Partitioning the ESX host

During the installation, manual partitioning is recommended for ESX 4.0 servers. There could be instances where the default partitioning could cause issues during the host's production life cycle; specifically, if the root file system fills up. With the capacity of today's drives in server class hardware, it shouldn't pose a problem.

If your host is going to be attached to a SAN, then set your partition sizes according to the table below (it will act as a good starting point and cover most needs). An explanation of each partition's function is included and provides a better understanding why the partitions are sized the way they are.

Mount Point	Type	Size (MB)	Partition Description	Physical Partition
/boot	EXT3	1100	The boot partition stores information required to boot the ESX Server hosts. For example, this is where the grub and LILO boot loaders reside.	X

	SWAP	1600	The swap partition allows ESX Server and third-party add-ons to use disk space when more memory is needed than the physical RAM allows.	
/	EXT3	5120	The root partition contains the ESX Server operating system and services, accessible through the Service Console. This partition also contains any third-party add-on services or applications you install.	
/home	EXT3	2048	This partition is used for storage by individual users.	
/tmp	EXT3	2048	This partition is used for storage of temporary files.	
/opt	EXT3	2048	This partition is used for 3rd party agents.	
/var	EXT3	4096	This partition is used for storage of log files, Service Console core dumps or other files used by third-party applications.	
	VMKCORE	110	The vmkcore partition is used to store core dumps for debugging and technical support.	X
	VMFS	Max Allowable	This partition is used for storing virtual machines and the Service Console vmdk.	X

/boot and VMKCORE are physical partitions. Remaining partitions are stored on a virtual disk called esxconsole-<system-uuid>/esxconsole.vmdk. The virtual disk is stored in a VMFS volume. The boot partition has grown from 250MB to 1100MB to make future upgrades to ESXi possible.

Adding more space to the /root partition?

Sizing your ESX host is very important. VMware states the minimum size for the root partition should be 5GB. In some cases (in the 2.x world) we made these partitions 2 or 2.5 GB and maybe that practice was fine for 2.x but now you need more space. The issue is that VMware does not support a way to increase the root partition size, but there are some ways to clean up or even add some space.

If you are running out of space or made your root partition smaller than it needs to be, there are things you can do.

- Check to see if you have any files or logs taking up space. You can use the find command from the COS.

    ```
    $ find / -size +10000k
    ```

    This will look for any files larger than 10MB. You can then delete or move those files. Inadvertently, a vmdk file may have been copied there temporally and was not deleted.

- You can use the ls -h command to show the file size in human-readable format such as 8K, 20MB, 1GB. You may want to use the -h option with the -s option. The -s will also show you the size of the files in blocks, not bytes. You can then move or delete files that are not needed.

- In building your ESX host if you did not specify a /var partition, your log files and core dumps will be placed in your /root partition. This means your log files or core dumps could be filling up your /root partition. Audit /var/log and /var/core on a regular base.

- If you cannot clean up your /root partition, you should rebuild your ESX host and size the partitions to VMware best practices.

- There is a sizing utility called GNU Parted that is not a VMware supported tool that can be used to resize the / root partition if there is space available on the disk.

Creating / Using an SMB mount point

At some point you may want to access a Windows share from your ESX server. To do this from the ESX console you basically need to mount (kind of like a drive mapping) the share to the ESX servers directory structure. The following steps will walk you through the process, assuming a share UNC that is \\WindowsServer\Share:

1. Create either a domain account or local server account and grant the account rights to the Windows share.

2. From the command line on the ESX Server as root, enable smbclient on the firewall:

    ```
    esxcfg-firewall --enableService smbClient
    ```

3. Create the mount point as root (a more meaningful name should be chosen):

```
mkdir /mnt/smbshare
```

4. To access the share:

```
mount -t smbfs -o
username=MyDomain\\MyUserID,password=MyDomainPasswor
d \\\\WindowsServer\\Share /mnt/smbshare
```

To shorten the command, a file can be created that contains the username and password for the Windows share. Keep in mind that the password will be stored in clear text. The file will need to have permission applied to it.

At the command line as root, type in the following commands to create the file:

```
1.  echo username=Domain\\User > ~root/.smbpasswd
2.  echo password=mySuperSecretPassword >> ~/.smbpasswd
3.  chmod 600 ~/.smbpasswd
4.  umount /mnt/smbshare
```

Make sure that you use a user name and password that has access to your share point. Now remount the share:

```
mount -t smbfs -o credentials=~root/.smbpasswd
\\\\WindowsServer\\Share /mnt/smbshare
```

 The mount point will go away after a reboot. To have the SMB share mounted during each reboot, follow the steps below.

As root, start your favorite editor (like nano) and save the following lines in /etc/init.d as smbshares:

```
#! /bin/sh
case "$1" in
  start)
    echo " Mounting SMB Shares..."
    mount /mnt/smbshare &>2
    ;;
  stop)
    echo " Unmounting SMB Shares..."
    umount /mnt/smbshare &>2
    ;;
esac
```

Change the permission to 755:

```
chmod 755 /etc/init.d/smbshares
```

Create link in rc3.d called S99smbshares to script in init.d:

```
ln -s /etc/init.d/smbshares S99smbshares
```

As root, open /etc/fstab in your favorite editor and enter the following line at the bottom (make sure that you enter everything on one line):

```
//server01/Software /mnt/smbshare smbfs
credentials=/root/.smbpasswd,gid=users 0 0
```

That's all there is to it. You now have a Windows file share available in the console after each reboot.

Lowering ESX memory requirements

For testing purposes it is possible to run ESX(i) within VMware Workstation or even nested within ESX(i) itself. In contrast to ESX(i) 3.x there's a minimum amount of memory(2GB) specified for ESX(i) 4.x. If the virtual machine does not meet the requirements the installation will fail. With the restriction of 4GB for most Laptop motherboards this would mean that it is impossible to run two virtual ESX hosts in a decent manner.

ESX:

1. Login to the Service Console

2. Edit the 00.vmnix file:
    `vi /etc/vmware/init/init.d/00.vmnix`

3. Change the following line to the desired value (we've successfully tested with 1.3GB):
    `RequiredMemory=2064384`

4. Save the file and exit vi.

5. Shutdown the ESX VM.

6. Reduce the memory of the ESX VM and start the VM.

ESXi:

1. Login to the console via "unsupported".

2. Edit the file /etc/vmware/esx.conf and add the following line:
    `/vmkernel/minMemoryCheck = "false"`

3. Save the file and exit vi.

4. Shutdown the ESXi VM.

5. Reduce the memory of the ESXi VM and start the VM.

Please note that "vi" is the preferred editor for these changes as any changes to the format of the file will leave the ESX(i) VM in an unbootable state.

Removing VMFS-2 drivers

When ESX 3 and VMFS 3.x was released many tried to unload the VMFS-2 module as documented in official VMware documentation. Unfortunately this wasn't a persistent solution and after a reboot the VMFS-2 module would be loaded again. As of ESX 4 this has been resolved, it is now possible to unload the VMFS-2 module in a persistent manner:

```
esxcfg-module –d vmfs2
```

HA, primary and secondary nodes

VMware HA uses primary and secondary nodes for replicating the state of the nodes and restarting VMs in case of an isolation/failure. VMware HA is a one click setup but in case issues occur it will come in handy knowing which node is primary and which node is secondary. For instance in a large environment with 8+ hosts in a cluster divided over two blade chassis it can be useful to know which hosts are primary if and when a chassis fails:

```
/opt/vmware/aam/bin/Cli
listnodes
```

With the CLI it is also possible to promote a node:

```
/opt/vmware/aam/bin/Cli
AAM> promotenode <nodename>
```

Or to demote a node to secondary:

```
/opt/vmware/aam/bin/Cli (ftcli on earlier versions)
AAM> demotenode <nodename>
```

Although this is a proven method it is, as far as we know, unsupported. Also keep in mind that the supported limit of primary nodes is 5. This is a soft limit, so you can manually add a 6th, but this is not supported nor recommended as the traffic required to keep the Database up to date will also grow faster with 6 or more than with 5.

Zipping up files on a host

Long before WinZip, there was gzip and tar. Gzip compresses or decompresses a file whereas tar or Tape ARchiver stores, lists or extracts multiple files in an archive.

If it's a single file, use gzip. For multiple ones, use tar. One important thing to remember about gzip is that, unlike tar, it replaces your original file with a compressed version.

Gzip also has different levels of compression: 1 being the least compressed and 9 being the maximum. It's also common to apply gzip to a tar file, which is why you sometimes see files with names like myfile.tar.gz. Below are common options for each command.

gzip

Compress: `gzip /vmfs/volumes/iso/myiso`

Uncompress: `gunzip /vmfs/volumes/iso/myiso.gz`

> Some common options
>
> ```
> -f - force
> -q - suppress all warning messages
> -v - verbose
> -n - Compression settings and speed(1 to 9)
> ```

tar

Compress: `tar -czvf logs.tgz /var/log`

Uncompress: `tar -xzvf myiso.tgz /vmfs/volumes/iso`

> Some common options
>
> ```
> c - create
> f - file
> t - test
> x - Extract
> z - uncompress
> v - verbose
> ```

For a gzipped, tar file you could do it all in one command:

```
tar xvzf myfiles.tar.gz
```

 If you would like to tar and gzip files on your Windows host, then you should download an app like WinRAR.

Working with antivirus software in the Service Console

If you have read the ESX Configuration Guide, on page 177, you would have noticed this:

> Also, try to run as few processes on the Service Console as possible. Ideally, strive to run only the essential processes, services, and agents such as virus checkers, virtual machine backups, and so forth.

The ESX 3.0 equivalent document contained a section that specifically stated that close attention should be paid to monitoring Service Console performance. Antivirus software can suck the life from your Service Console and eventually your ability to mange the environment. However, organizations operate in a "Risk Avoidance" atmosphere. If you must run antivirus software in the Service Console, you should consider the following:

- If possible, disable real-time monitoring or lower the priority of the process.

- At a minimum, exclude all virtual machine files from being scanned. Better yet, exclude every VMFS volume from being scanned.

- Avoid doing full system scans during peak times and limit the number of files being scanned simultaneously.

We do not recommend installing antivirus scanners in the Service Console. We recommend taking all necessary precautions in terms of root access (disable root access, enable sudo and sudoerslist) and security hardening.

Tripwire released a freeware tool that scans your ESX host for exploits. This tool includes a great PDF with all the remediations for these exploits. (http://www.vwire.com/) The tool has been developed with VMware and contains many of the tips found in the VMware Infrastructure Security Hardening Guide.

Short of pulling ESX servers off the network and encasing them in concrete, the least amount of security you should do is to limit access to the server (both physically and to the Service Console). Keep the firewall enabled with only the needed ports opened.

Virtual Machines

vSphere 4.0 introduces Virtual Machine hardware version 7 and with that a number of new features for virtual machines. This section will introduce those features and review a number of procedures for managing your virtual machines.

What's New

8-Way Virtual SMP

vSphere 4.0 increases the virtual CPU limit to 8 from 4 to allow a virtual machine (VM) to run on up to 8 logical processors on your host. You can select any number of CPUs for your VM between 1 and 8, but the host must have at least the same number of logical processors and to exceed 5 virtual CPUs (vCPUs) the host must be licensed at the Enterprise Plus level. The VM must also be running at hardware version 7 to use more than 4 vCPUs.

When creating a new VM on a multiprocessor host you will be presented with the Virtual CPUs page on which you can select the number of virtual CPUs to assign to the VM. If you are unable to assign more than 4 vCPUs then you should check your licensing for the host as well as ensuring that it has the required number of logical processors. You can also edit an existing VM to change the number of vCPUs assigned to it.

1. Ensure that the VM is powered down.

2. In the vSphere Client, right click on the VM and select Edit Settings …

3. On the Hardware tab select the CPUs device and then change the Number of virtual processors settings to the number of vCPUs that you desire for the VM.

PowerCLI Example

The following shows how PowerCLI can be used to alter the number of vCPUs for a virtual machine:

```
Cmdlets
Set-VM

Related Cmdlets
Get-VM
Move-VM
New-VM
Remove-VM
Start-VM
Stop-VM
```

Suspend-VM

EXAMPLE 1:
Alters an existing VM named PROD1 to change the current number
of vCPUs to 8:

Get-VM PROD1 | Set-VM -NumCpu 8

When setting the vCPU count for the VM keep in mind that it is best
for VM and overall host performance to start with one vCPU and
increase the count only if the VM demonstrates a need for additional
vCPUs. If you are changing the vCPU count from 1 to 2 or more keep
in mind that you may have to update the guest OS to support multiple
CPUs. If your host is licensed at vSphere Advanced or higher level and
the guest OS supports hot add CPU, you can also change the vCPU
count while the guest OS is running. See the Guest Operating System
Installation Guide for a list of guest OSes that support this feature -
http://www.vmware.com/pdf/GuestOS_guide.pdf.

255 GB RAM per VM

The VM memory limit has been increased from 64 to 255 GB in all
editions of vSphere. The memory for a VM can be set when creating a
VM in the vSphere Client. On the Memory screen of the Create New
Virtual Machine wizard you can set a value of the VMs memory in 4 MB
increments up to 255 GB. You can also change the memory for an
existing VM.

1. Ensure that the VM is powered down.

2. In the vSphere Client, right click on the VM and select Edit
    Settings …

3. On the Hardware tab select the Memory device. Change the
    Memory Size for the VM to have the amount of memory
    that you desire for this VM.

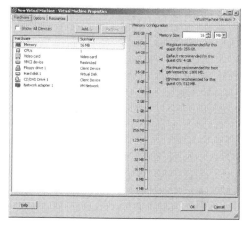

PowerCLI Example

The following shows how PowerCLI can be used to alter the amount of
memory for a virtual machine:

Cmdlets
```
Set-VM
```

Related Cmdlets
```
Get-VM
Move-VM
New-VM
Remove-VM
Start-VM
Stop-VM
Suspend-VM
```

EXAMPLE 1:
```
Alters an existing VM named PROD1 to change the current amount
of memory to 255GB:

Get-VM PROD1 | Set-VM -MemoryMB (255GB / 1MB)
```

If you are trying to add more than 64 GB of memory, but are shown a
maximum of 64 GB for the VM, ensure that the VM has been upgraded
to hardware version 7. Also note that the guest OS may have a limit on
it which may prevent it from using the memory that you assign to it. For
example with Windows 2008 Enterprise x86 the OS memory limit is 64
GB. Assigning 128 GB to this VM will not enable the guest OS to use
all 128 GB.

Enhanced Clustering Support for Windows 2000, 2003 and 2008

vSphere provides enhanced support for Windows clustering both with 32-bit and 64-bit guests. Boot from FC SAN is now supported for clusters as well as Majority Node Set clusters with application-level redirection. Setup of Windows clusters on vSphere is covered in detail in VMware's setup document (http://www.vmware.com/pdf/vsphere4/r40/vsp_40_mscs.pdf) but there are a number of important items to note about newly supported items and limitations in vSphere's Windows cluster support.

vSphere Clustering Support Requirements

1. Windows 2000 and 2003 require the use of the LSI Logic Parallel virtual SCSI adapter and Windows 2008 requires use of the LSI Logic SAS adapter.

2. The default virtual NIC type should be used for all Windows versions.

3. The disk time out value at HKEY_LOCAL_MACHINE\CurrentControlSet\Services\Disk\TimeOutValue should be set to 60 seconds or more. Creation of a cluster can reset this value, so it should be checked after creation of your cluster.

4. When creating a virtual disk for use in the cluster, it should be created with the option "Support clustering features such as Fault Tolerance". This will create the disks with a eagerzerodthick format.

5. Virtual NICs should be added to the VMs prior to adding your clustered storage. This will prevent virtual NICs from moving to a new PCI slot as described in this KB article - http://kb.vmware.com/kb/1513.

6. The cluster should be limited to 2 nodes.

7. You should configure your cluster nodes to synchronize time with a common time server. Host based time synchronization should be disabled. This can be done by opening the VMware Tools icon in Control Panel, and un checking the "Time synchronization between the virtual machine and the ESX Server operating system" option.

vSphere Clustering Support Limitations and Restrictions

1. Virtual compatibility mode (non pass through RDM) is not supported when clustering Windows 2008 across ESX hosts.

2. While it is supported to have the guest boot disk on FC SAN, it is not supported to boot from iSCSI SAN.

3. Clustering is not supported on iSCSI or NFS disks.

4. When clustering across ESX hosts, both hosts must be running the same version of ESX or ESXi.

5. You cannot enable VMware Fault Tolerance on clustered VMs.

6. The VMs must be running hardware version 7.

7. VMotion is not supported with Microsoft clustering.

8. N-Port ID Virtualization (NPIV) is not supported.

9. Round robin is not supported as the path policy when using native multi-pathing.

10. Clustered VMs cannot be part of a VMware HA or DRS cluster.

PowerCLI Example

The following shows how PowerCLI can be used to enable and disable Fault Tolerance:

```
Cmdlets
Get-VM
Get-View
```

```
Related Cmdlets
Get-VM
Move-VM
New-VM
Remove-VM
Start-VM
Stop-VM
Suspend-VM
Get-VIObjectByVIView
```

```
EXAMPLE 1:
Enables Fault Tolerance on a VM called PROD1, this
example chooses the host to place the FT VM.

Get-VM PROD1 | Get-View | ForEach-Object {
$_.CreateSecondaryVM($null) }
```

```
EXAMPLE 2:
Disables Fault Tolerance on a VM called PROD1.

Get-VM PROD1 | Select -First 1 | Get-View | ForEach-
Object { $_.TurnOffFaultToleranceForVM() }
```

Virtual Machine Hot-Add Support

vSphere 4 introduces hot-add support for PCI devices such as storage, network and USB controllers. Also added is support for the hot-adding of CPU and memory. The VM must be at hardware version 7. The guest OS must also support hot-add. With the general release of vSphere, hot-add for PCI devices is widely supported by the guest OSes that vSphere supports, hot-add memory is supported by far fewer guest OSes and hot-add CPU support is only available for a few guest types. To add a PCI device or storage to your VM,

1. Right click on the VM while it is running and select Edit Settings …

2. On the Hardware tab click on Add.

3. Select the type of PCI device to add and then complete the Add Hardware wizard.

To hot-add CPU or memory to the VM, follow this process.

1. Ensure that the VM is powered down.

2. In the vSphere Client, right click on the VM and select Edit Settings …

3. Select the Options tab and look for the Memory/CPU Hotplug setting under Advanced. If the setting is not available, then the guest OS type is set to an OS that does not support either feature.

4. For hot-add memory check the "Enable memory hot add for this machine" option. For hot-add CPU you can pick either "Enable CPU hot add only for this machine" or "Enable CPU hot add and remove for this virtual machine".

5. After the VM is powered on, you will have to select Edit Settings … again to hot-add memory or CPU.

6. On the Hardware tab, you will be able to edit the memory or CPU count depending on the capabilities of the guest OS.

When hot-adding resources to your VM, you may find that a reboot or further system configuration is required in the VM for the new hardware to be fully usable. With hot-add memory and CPU you may experience temporary performance fluctuations as the guest OS begins to use the new resources. The described hot-add features are available in vSphere Advanced and higher.

Hot Extend for Virtual Disk

With vSphere you can now extend a VMFS virtual disk. The disk must be in persistent mode and not have any snapshots.

1. In the vSphere Client, right click on the VM and select Edit Settings …

2. Select the virtual hard disk to expand and then enter the final size that you want the virtual hard disk to be.

3.   Click OK to commit the change.

After you have made the change, you will have to reconfigure your guest
OS to recognize the additional space. This feature is available with
vSphere Standard and higher. The maximum size that you will be able
to extend the virtual disk that is on a VMFS datastore will depend on
the block size that the datastore was formatted with and not the free
space available. For a VMFS datastore with a 1 MB block size, you will
only be able to extend the virtual hard disk to 256 GB regardless of the
free space on the datastore.

New Virtual Hardware

As mentioned above, vSphere introduces hardware version 7. Along
with some of the features already discussed hardware version 7 includes
the following new hardware features.

1.   Up to 16 virtual PCI devices which allows for combinations
with up to 4 virtual SCSI adapters connected to up to 60
virtual SCSI hard disks, 10 virtual NICs, 10 video displays,
or 2 VMDirectPath PCI / PCIe devices.

2.   The LSI Logic SAS virtual SCSI adapter which provides
support for Windows 2008 Failover Clusters.

3.   An IDE virtual hard disk which allow a VM to have up to 4
virtual IDE hard disks to support guest OSes that may not
have the appropriate SCSI driver to run one of VMware's
SCSI virtual adapters.

4.   The 3rd generation paravirtualized NIC from VMware –
VMXNET3. VMXNET3 includes the following
improvements over VMXNET2 (Enhanced).

a.   VLAN off-loading

b.   IPv6 checksum and TCP Segmentation
Offloading (TSO) over IPv6

c.   Message-signaled interrupts (MSI) / MSI-X
support which provides a performance
enhancement over traditional line-based
interrupts. This feature does require guest OS
support of MSI / MSI-X.

d.   Receive-Side Scaling (RSS) is supported on
Windows 2008. RSS technology enables efficient
distribution of network receive processing over
multiple CPUs in multiprocessor VMs. In
Windows 2008, right click on the VMXNET3
virtual NIC and select Properties. Click on the

Configure button for the virtual NIC and on the Advanced tab change the RSS setting from Disabled to Enabled.

e.   Large TX / RX ring sizes. With Enhanced VMXNET, the default number of transmit and receive buffers were 256 and 150, with a maximum value of 512. These settings could be changed by editing the configuration (VMX) file for the VM. With VMXNET3 and E1000, the maximum values for transmit and receive buffers are now 4096. The settings are also controlled by the driver in the guest OS. For Windows the values for the E1000 driver can be updated by setting the Receive Buffers and Transmit Buffers properties on the Advanced tab of the Properties screen for the virtual adapter. For Linux, you can use ethtool to update the values for both E1000 and VMXNET3 virtual NICs.

5.   The VMware Paravirtualized SCSI (PVSCSI) virtual adapter is a high performance adapter which lowers CPU utilization and increases IO throughput for VMs. This adapter is recommended for high performance SAN environments in which disk I/O to the VM will exceed 5000 IOPS. The PVSCSI adapter requires the installation of VMware Tools and thus should not be used for the VMs boot disk. Rather you should create the VM with a boot disk that uses the default virtual SCSI adapter, and then add additional storage attached to a PVSCSI adapter.

When creating new VMs on vSphere, hardware version 7 is the default option for VMs. It is still possible to create hardware version 4 VMs which will be compatible with ESX 3.0 or later. When creating a new VM, select the Custom configuration option and you will then get the Virtual Machine Version screen on which you can pick between version 4 and 7. VMs created with hardware version 7 cannot be run on ESX / ESXi releases prior to version 4.0.

The new hardware options can be enabled when creating a new VM or after by editing the settings for a VM.

1.   In the vSphere Client select File \ New \ Virtual Machine …

2.   Choose the Custom configuration option on the first screen of the wizard.

3.   On the Network screen you will be able to select VMXNET 3 as the network adapter type. Keep in mind that the guest

OS will not be able to use the VMXNET3 NIC until
VMware Tools has been installed into the guest OS.

4. On the SCSI Controller screen you will be able to select
    between BusLogic Parallel, LSI Logic Parallel, LSI Logic
    SAS or VMware Paravirtual. As with the VMXNET3 NIC,
    the PVSCSI adapter will require the install of VMware tools
    for the device to work with the guest OS.

5. After setting the options on the Create a Disk screen, you
    will be able to specify if the virtual hard disk should be
    connected to the virtual SCSI adapter or be added as an IDE
    virtual disk.

6. On the Ready to Complete screen you can also check the
    "Edit the virtual machine settings before completion"
    option to add additional devices and settings to the VM.

If you have already created your VM, you can edit the settings for the
VM to use these new virtual hardware features. As previously noted,
some devices will require changes within the guest OS to function
properly.

1. In the vSphere Client, right click on the VM and select Edit
    Settings ... It is possible to add these devices while your VM
    is powered on if your vSphere install is licensed for hot-add
    and the guest OS supports this feature.

2. To change video settings select the Video card device. You
    can then set the number of video displays between 1 and 10.
    You can also set a fixed amount for video card memory, set
    the desired resolution and color depth for the displays or set
    vSphere to automatically determine the video card memory
    required. The "Enable 3D Support" option is not supported
    on vSphere and is grayed out.

3. To add a VMXNET3 NIC, click on Add and then select
    Ethernet Adapter on the Device Type screen. On the
    Network Connection screen you can set the Adapter Type
    to VMXNET3.

4. To add the PVSCSI adapter to a system already configured
    with another adapter type and virtual disk select Add on the
    Hardware tab and then Hard Disk on the Device Type
    screen. On the Advanced Options screen, select a SCSI ID
    that does not correspond to an existing virtual SCSI adapter.
    Complete the Add Hardware Wizard. On the Hardware tab
    you will see "New SCSI Controller (adding)" in the list of
    devices. Select that device and then click on Change Type to
    change the adapter to a VMware Paravirtual controller type.

Keep in mind that changing the controller type for the VM's boot device may render the VM unbootable. The VM should be powered down when making a change to the adapter type.

5. To add an IDE virtual disk, click on Add on the Hardware tab. Select Hard Disk as the device type. On the Advanced Options screen, change the Virtual Device Node setting from SCSI to IDE and choose a free IDE device number.

VMDirectPath

VMDirectPath I/O device access reduces CPU overhead when dealing with VM workloads that require constant access to I/O devices by allowing your VM to directly access a hardware device. VMDirectPath is fully supported for the following network devices:

1. Broadcom 57710 10 Gigabit Ethernet Controller

2. Broadcom 57711 10 Gigabit Ethernet Controller

3. Intel 82598 10 Gigabit Ethernet Controller

VMDirectPath is experimentally supported with these storage controllers:

1. LSI 3442e-R 3Gb SAS

2. LSI 3801e (1068-chip based) 3Gb SAS

3. QLogic QLA25xx 8Gb Fibre Channel

4. Emulex LPe12000 8Gb Fibre Channel

While the number of items supported is minimal at this time, VMDirectPath has been found to work with a number of devices such as PCI fax cards. VMDirectPath has certain requirements of the host and is currently only supported on Intel 5500 systems. These systems come with a feature called I/O memory management unit that will need to be enabled in the BIOS of the host. In the BIOS of an Intel server, this option may be listed as Intel Virtual Technology for Directed I/O (VT-d). VMDirectPath is experimentally supported on AMD systems that have I/O Virtualization Technology (AMD IOMMU).

Each VM can connect to two VMDirectPath devices and a device used for VMDirectPath cannot be shared with any other VMs. Enabling VMDirectPath for a VM also disables the following features: Memory Overcommitment, page sharing, hot add/remove of virtual devices, suspend and resume, Record and Replay, High Availability, Fault Tolerance and VMotion. A VMDirectPath VM can be part of a DRS cluster, but it cannot be migrated between hosts.

Enabling VMDirectPath for a VM involves both configuration of the host and the VM. To setup a PCI device for VMDirectPath

1. In the vSphere Client select the host, choose the Configuration tab and then select Advanced Settings in the Hardware Section. If the host supports VMDirectPath path you should see the message that "No devices are currently enabled for passthrough".

2. Click on Configure Passthrough ...

3. Select the devices that you want to enable for VMDirectPath. In some cases, a reboot of the host may be required to make the device available to a VM via VMDirectPath. A message will be shown on the VMDirectPath configuration screen should this be the case.

Once your devices have been enabled for VMDirectPath, you can add these to your host.

1. Ensure that the VM has been powered down. VMDirectPath devices cannot be added to a VM while it is powered on.

2. In the vSphere Client, right click on the VM and select Edit Settings ...

3. On the Hardware tab select Add and then select PCI Device as the Device Type to add.

4. On the select PCI/PCIe Device screen select the PCI device to add to the VM.

5. Complete the wizard and then boot the VM to perform any guest OS configuration for the device.

Note that when you add a PCI device to a VM, the memory reservation for the VM will be set to equal the amount of memory assigned to the VM and that as mentioned above certain features will no longer be available for this VM.

Virtual Machine Communication Interface (VMCI)

vSphere adds the VMCI device which was designed to allow for high speed communication between the VM and host or between VMs on the same host. The VMware VMCI sockets library provides an API similar to using the Windows socket interface or the Berkeley UNIX socket interface. VMCI does not have any dependencies on the networking setup in the VM to operate. Information about updating applications to use VMCI can be found in this PDF - http://www.vmware.com/support/developer/vmci-sdk/ws65_s2_esx4_vmci_sockets.pdf.

If you enable VMCI for a VM, you should note that existing VMCI sockets will not survive the VMotion of a VM and that VMCI sockets will stop working when a VM is enabled for Fault Tolerance. The VMCI device is available in a VM once it is upgraded to hardware version 7. By default the VMCI device that will exist in a VM will allow VM to host communication. VM to VM VMCI communication is disabled by default. To enable VMCI between VMs

1. Ensure that the VM is powered down.

2. In the vSphere Client, right click on the VM and select Edit Settings …

3. Select the VMCI device and check the option "Enable VMCI between VMs". The VMCI device should now have a summary description of Unrestricted.

Multicore Support in Virtual Machines

When creating a VM with 4 vCPUs the guest OS will see each vCPU as a distinct CPU. For a guest OS limited to two physical CPUs, you will only be able to run the guest with 2 vCPUs even though the host may have 2 physical CPUs with a total of 4 to 8 CPU cores. To assign multicore CPUs to such a guest it is possible with the configuration parameter cpuid.coresPerSocket.

1. Ensure that the VM is powered down.

2. In the vSphere Client, right click on the VM and select Edit Settings …

3. Select the Options tab.

4. Click on General item of the Advanced section

5. Select Configuration Parameters …

6. Click Add Row.

7. Enter the value cpuid.coresPerSocket in the name column and enter a value of 2 4 or 8.

8. Click Ok to close the Properties window.

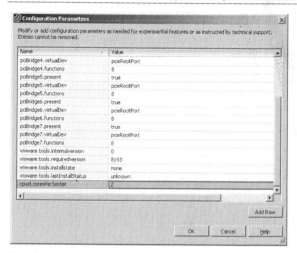

The value entered for cpuid.coresPerSocket must divide evenly into the number of vCPUs assigned to the VM. If you have an 8 vCPU VM and assign a value to cpuid.coresPerSocket of 2, then the guest OS will see four dual core CPUs. Note that this feature only has experimental support in the general release of vSphere and is not intended to circumvent any CPU licensing restrictions imposed by your software vendors. Once you have made this change you can verify it by running a utility like CPU Z - http://www.cpuid.com/cpuz.php in the VM.

Upgrading Virtual Machines

If you are upgrading from ESX/ESXi 3.5 you will want to upgrade VMware Tools and the virtual hardware version of your VM. When creating new VMs with vSphere, the default hardware version will be 7 so you won't have to upgrade the hardware version, but occasionally you will want to upgrade the version of VMware Tools as VMware releases updates and patches for vSphere. VMware Tools is a suite of utilities and drivers that improve the performance and management of your VMs. It is not required for running a guest OS, but you will not have the best performance and will lose functionality without VMware Tools.

VMware Tools for Linux, Windows, Solaris and NetWare are stored on the vSphere host as ISO images. When you want to install VMware Tools into a VM, the host will mount the ISO image into the guest OS and run the installation on the ISO image. When VMware Tools is upgraded, a complete uninstall and reinstall is performed of the install package. In some cases functionality such as networking might be temporarily interrupted during the upgrade, but should be restored after the upgrade is complete.

The upgrade of the virtual machine hardware version from version 4 to 7 is necessary to take advantage of new features in vSphere. If upgrading from virtual hardware version 3, the upgrade is a non-reversible action. If the VM is running version 4, then it is possible to reverse the process if you take a virtual machine backup or snapshot before you upgrade the virtual hardware. If you perform the upgrade with vCenter Update Manager then an automatic backup is performed as part of the hardware version upgrade. It is necessary to power down the VM to upgrade the virtual hardware version. It is also possible to upgrade both VMware Tools and the hardware version in a single step. The following pages will outline methods to both manually and automatically upgrade both VMware Tools and the VM hardware version. When planning to upgrade VMware Tools or the hardware version of your VMs, you should plan for some downtime. The upgrade of both components in a Windows VM would require a total of two shutdown and power on operations. The first shutdown would be required after VMware Tools was upgraded and the second would occur after Windows had detected new hardware following the upgrade of the hardware version for the VM. For Linux, Netware and Solaris guests, a single shutdown and power on would be required to upgrade the virtual hardware version and VMware Tools.

While these upgrades are a relatively safe operation, a backup of your VMs is recommended before proceeding with these upgrades. As mentioned, an upgrade of the virtual hardware version for a VM is not always a reversible process.

For most installations of VMware Tools selecting "Typical" will install the virtual hardware and tools needed to run a VM on vSphere. If you feel that you need additional features or need to select only specific aspects of the upgrade you will want to consult the VMware documentation for a greater understanding of what each option entails.

 It may be necessary to reconfigure your network adapters after upgrading VMware tools (major upgrades sometimes do this). The network adapters may be detected as newly installed hardware and of course this means your IP info goes the way of the dinosaur and you need to re-add the IP info to the "new" adapter.

Manually Upgrade VMware Tools for Microsoft Windows

1. Ensure that the VM is powered on.

2. Select the VM in the vSphere Client and then look at the Summary tab. The VMware Tools label in the General section will tell you if VMware Tools is not installed, installed but out of date or installed and current.

3. Right click on the VM, select Guest and then Install/Upgrade VMware Tools.

4. Select the Interactive Tools Upgrade option and then access the console of the VM and login if necessary.

5. The VMware Tools ISO image for Windows should be mounted to the CD-ROM for the VM. If autorun is enabled in the guest, the install for VMware Tools will start automatically. If that is not the case then open the drive for the CD-ROM and run setup.exe.

6. Follow the installation prompts for VMware Tools. A typical install is appropriate for a Windows VM running on vSphere.

7. After the install or upgrade is complete, you will be prompted to restart the VM. After the VM has rebooted, the VMware Tools label on the Summary tab for the VM should display a status of OK.

Manually Upgrade VMware Tools for Linux in an X Terminal

Note that this process requires the RPM installer which is not available as part of ESXi. Only the tar installer is available and thus you should use the tar installer process found below.

1. Ensure that the VM is powered on.

2. Select the VM in the vSphere Client and then look at the Summary tab. The VMware Tools label in the General section will tell you if VMware Tools is not installed, installed but out of date or installed and current.

3. Right click on the VM, select Guest and then Install/Upgrade VMware Tools.

4. Select the Interactive Tools Upgrade option and then access the console of the VM and login if necessary.

5.   If the VMware Tools CD icon appears double click to start the upgrade process or should the file manager window open, double click on the RPM installer. Should neither appear, open a command prompt and start the RPM installer manually

6.   If prompted for the root password, enter it and click OK.

7.   On the Completed System Preparation screen click Continue. The installer for VMware Tools will complete without a finish or confirmation message.

8.   In a terminal window, switch to the root login with su – and run the command vmware-config-tools.pl to configure VMware Tools.

9.   After the configuration of VMware Tools is complete, run the below commands to restore the network.

/etc/init.d/network stop

rmmod vmxnet

modprode vmxnet

/etc/init.d/network start

10.   Logout of the VM, close the console and verify that the VMware Tools label on the Summary tab has a status of OK.

Manually Upgrade VMware Tools for Linux with the RPM Installer

1.   Ensure that the VM is powered on.

2.   Select the VM in the vSphere Client and then look at the Summary tab. The VMware Tools label in the General section will tell you if VMware Tools is not installed, installed but out of date or installed and current.

3.   Right click on the VM, select Guest and then Install/Upgrade VMware Tools.

4.   Select the Interactive Tools Upgrade option and then access the console of the VM and login if necessary.

5.   In the console switch to the root login if necessary with su -.

6.   Create the folder /mnt/cdrom with the command mkdir /mnt/cdrom if it does not exist

7. If your Linux distribution does not automatically mount CD-ROMs, you can do so with a command similar to mount /dev/cdrom /mnt/cdrom

8. Change to a working directory with a command like cd /tmp

9. Extract the RPM installer with a command like rpm –Uhv /mount/cdrom/VMwareTools-4.0.0-<xxxxxx>.i386.rpm. <xxxxxx> will reflect the build number for the VMware Tools package.

10. Double click on the RPM installer file to start the installation.

11. When the install is complete, run ./usr/bin/vmware-config-tools.pl to configure VMware Tools.

12. After the configuration of VMware Tools is complete, run the below commands to restore the network.

> /etc/init.d/network stop
>
> rmmod vmxnet
>
> modprode vmxnet
>
> /etc/init.d/network start

13. Unmount the CD-ROM image with the command umount /dev/cdrom.

14. Logout of the VM, close the console and verify that the VMware Tools label on the Summary tab has a status of OK.

Manually Upgrade VMware Tools for Linux with the TAR Installer

1. Ensure that the VM is powered on.

2. Select the VM in the vSphere Client and then look at the Summary tab. The VMware Tools label in the General section will tell you if VMware Tools is not installed, installed but out of date or installed and current.

3. Right click on the VM, select Guest and then Install/Upgrade VMware Tools.

4. Select the Interactive Tools Upgrade option and then access the console of the VM and login if necessary.

5. In the console switch to the root login if necessary with su -.

6. Create the folder /mnt/cdrom with the command mkdir /mnt/cdrom if it does not exist

7. If your Linux distribution does not automatically mount CD-ROMs, you can do so with a command similar to mount /dev/cdrom /mnt/cdrom

8. Change to a working directory with a command like cd /tmp

15. Extract the tar package with a command like tar zxpf /mnt/cdrom/VMwareTools-4.0.0. -<xxxxxx>.tar.gz. <xxxxxx> will reflect the build number for the VMware Tools package.

16. Start the tar installer by entering the following commands cd vmware-tools-distrib and ./vmware-install.pl

17. Answer the prompts that the install process presents. In most cases pressing Enter to accept the default values will be sufficient. Then follow the instructions at the end of the script.

18. After the configuration of VMware Tools is complete, run the below commands to restore the network.

   /etc/init.d/network stop

   rmmod vmxnet

   modprode vmxnet

   /etc/init.d/network start

19. Unmount the CD-ROM image with the command umount /dev/cdrom.

20. Logout of the VM, close the console and verify that the VMware Tools label on the Summary tab has a status of OK.

Automatically Upgrade VMware Tools for Windows and Linux VMs

When you choose the option to automatically upgrade VMware Tools, you do not need to interact with the VM to perform the upgrade. The upgrade process will uninstall the prior version of VMware Tools and then install the latest version that is available on your vSphere host. For a Windows VM the reboot required at the end of the install of VMware

Tools will be automatically performed. The automatic upgrade option is not available for Netware or Solaris VMs.

1. Ensure that the VM in which you want to upgrade VMware Tools is powered on.

2. Select the VM in the vSphere Client and then look at the Summary tab. The VMware Tools label in the General section will tell you if VMware Tools is not installed, installed but out of date or installed and current.

3. Right click on the VM, select Guest and then Install/Upgrade VMware Tools.

4. Select the option Automatic Tools Upgrade.

5. For a Windows guest, you can also specify a location for the log file that will be generated. Enter the value /l "path\file.log" in the Advanced Option field.

6. For a Linux VM run the below commands once the upgrade is complete.

    /etc/init.d/network stop

    rmmod vmxnet

    modprode vmxnet

    /etc/init.d/network start

7. Verify that the VMware Tools label on the Summary tab has a status of OK.

Configure a VM to Automatically Upgrade VMware Tools

You can configure a VM to check and install a VMware Tools upgrade each time you power on the VM. This option is available for Linux and Windows VMs.

1. Ensure that the VM is powered off.

2. In the vSphere Client, right click on the VM and select Edit Settings …

3. Select the Options tab and then VMware Tools.

4. Check the advanced option "Check and upgrade Tools before each power-on" and then click OK.

When you next power on the VM, a check will be made of the version of VMware Tools that is running and if necessary an upgrade will be run. A Windows VM will be automatically rebooted after the upgrade process has completed.

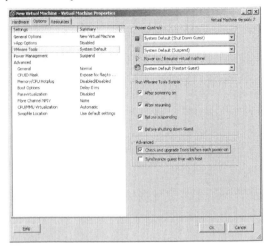

Upgrade VMware Tools on Multiple VMs

Use the following procedure to upgrade many Linux or Windows VMs at the same time. Windows VMs will automatically reboot once the upgrade process is complete.

1. In the vSphere Client select the host or cluster containing the VMs to upgrade.

2. Ensure that the VMs are powered on.

3. Select the VMs to upgrade, right click and select Install/Upgrade Tools.

4. For a Linux VM run the below commands once the upgrade is complete.

    /etc/init.d/network stop

    rmmod vmxnet

    modprode vmxnet

/etc/init.d/network start

5. Verify that the VMware Tools label on the Summary tab has a status of OK.

PowerCLI Example

The following shows how PowerCLI can be used to manipulate the VMware Tools installer:

```
Cmdlets
Update-Tools
Mount-Tools
Dismount-Tools
Get-VM
```

```
Related Cmdlets
Set-VM
Move-VM
New-VM
Remove-VM
Start-VM
Stop-VM
Suspend-VM
```

```
EXAMPLE 1:
Upgrade VMware Tools on all VMs:

Get-VM | Update-Tools
```

```
EXAMPLE 2:
Upgrade VMware Tools on a single virtual machine called PROD1:

Get-VM PROD1 | Update-Tools
```

```
EXAMPLE 3:
List all virtual machines and their version of VMTools:

$VMTools = @()
Foreach ($VM in (Get-VM)){
        $MyDetails = "" | Select-Object Name, Tools
        $MyDetails.Name = $vm.Name
        $MyDetails.Tools = $vm.config.tools.toolsVersion
        $VMTools += $MyDetails
}
$VMTools
```

Upgrading Virtual Hardware

To take advantage of the latest features in vSphere, the VM must be running VM hardware version 7. For VMs upgraded from ESX / ESXi 3.5, these will be running version 4.

1. Create a backup or snapshot of your VM. If you're using vCenter Update Manager then the backup will happen automatically. The backup or snapshot will allow you to

revert to hardware version 4 if necessary. It is not possible to revert back if upgrading from hardware version 3.

2. Ensure that VMware Tools is upgraded. This is particularly helpful on Windows VMs to help prevent the loss of network settings.

3. Ensure that no suspend file exists and that at least one virtual disk exists.

4. Power off the VM.

5. In the vSphere client, right click on the VM and select Upgrade Virtual Hardware. This option will not be visible if the VM is already at hardware version 7.

6. Click Yes when prompted to continue the upgrade.

7. Power on the VM. For a Windows VM the guest OS will detect new hardware and require a reboot.

8. Once the process is complete, the Summary tab for the VM should show a value of 7 for the VM Version label.

It is possible to upgrade the hardware version on more than one VM at a time.

1. In the vSphere Client select the host or cluster containing the VMs to upgrade.

2. Ensure that the VMs are powered off.

3. Select the VMs to upgrade, right click and select Upgrade Virtual Hardware and then select Yes.

4. Power on the VMs. For a Windows VM the guest OS will detect new hardware and require a reboot.

5. Once the process is complete, the Summary tabs for the VMs should show a value of 7 for the VM Version label.

---

 vCenter Server 4.0 includes vmware-vmupgrade.exe which allows for the mass update of virtual hardware or VMware Tools. Usage of the command is documented in KB article http://kb.vmware.com/kb/1003966. Use of the command to upgrade VMware Tools or virtual hardware is not recommended by VMware.

PowerCLI Example

The following shows how PowerCLI can be used to update the hardware version to V7:

```
Cmdlets
Get-VM
Get-View
Get-Cluster
```

```
Related Cmdlets
Set-VM
Move-VM
New-VM
Remove-VM
Start-VM
Stop-VM
Suspend-VM
Get-VIObjectByVIView
Move-Cluster
New-Cluster
Remove-Cluster
Set-Cluster
```

EXAMPLE 1:
Upgrade hardware version for a virtual machine named PROD1:

```
Get-VM PROD1 | Get-View | ForEach-Object { $_.UpgradeVM($null)
}
```

EXAMPLE 2:
Upgrade hardware version for all virtual machines in a cluster named Non-Production:

```
Get-Cluster "Non-Production" | Get-VM | Get-View | ForEach-
Object { $_.UpgradeVM($null) }
```

Using VMware Tools Scripts

Part of the installation of VMware Tools is the addition of certain scripts that can be run during specific power operations. The scripts will be run for the following events:

1. After powering on

2. After resuming

3. Before suspending

4. Before shutting down Guest.

For a Windows guest these scripts are located in C:\Program Files\VMware\VMware Tools and for Linux in /etc/vmware-tools. These scripts can be used to manage special procedures for applications running within your VM to ensure that a VM power operation does not negatively impact your application. These scripts require the install of

VMware Tools and any custom scripts that you create should be stored on the hard disk for the VM. If you want to add a custom script, you should not edit the VMware supplied files as these will be overwritten the next time VMware Tools is upgraded. To setup your own custom script

1. Create a batch script you wish to run and place the file on the hard disk for the VM.

2. Open the Control Panel in the VM and then open the VMware Tools applet

3. With the VMware Tools Properties window open, click on the scripts tab.

4. Choose the event that this script will run for.

5. Select the Custom Script option and the browse to find your custom script.

6. Click on OK to save your changes.

To ensure that scripts will be run for the 4 power operations

1. In the vSphere Client, right click on the VM and select Edit Settings …

2. Select Option tab and the VMware Tools.

3. Enable the corresponding events in the Run VMware Tools Scripts section.

 These events only work when using the Power Control buttons for the virtual machine. Also, a restart does not kick off the power on or power off script.

VM Startup and Shutdown Configuration

Controlling the automatic startup and shutdown of a VM can be helpful in some environments to ease the task load when patching and maintaining hosts. With the appropriate settings, a host can be configured to start VMs in a certain order when it boots up or to shutdown guest OSes in a graceful manner during a power outage.

By default VMs on your vSphere host will be set to manual startup. To change the startup and shutdown settings

1. In the vSphere client select the host and then the Configuration tab.

2. Select the Virtual Machine Startup/Shutdown link to display settings for that host.

3. Select the Properties… link in the upper right corner to open the Virtual Machine Startup and Shutdown screen.

4. Ensure that the option "Allow virtual machines to start and stop automatically with the system" is checked.

5. You can then set the Default Startup Delay options if desired, but the defaults will be sufficient for most cases. You can also set the Default Shutdown Delay time and if desired the Shutdown Action to perform (Guest Shutdown, Power Off or Suspend).

6. Select a VM and then click the Move Up or Move Down buttons to move the VM to the appropriate start up group. With a critical VM like a domain controller, you may wish to set the VM to be in the Automatic Startup group with an order of 1. For less critical VMs, you may find the Any Order startup group sufficient.

7. You can also edit a specific VM to change the startup or shutdown delay should that VM need extra time to perform those operations.

8. Click the OK to save your configuration.

PowerCLI Example

The following shows how PowerCLI can be used to alter the startup policy of the virtual machines:

Cmdlets
```
Get-VMStartPolicy
Set-VMStartPolicy
```

EXAMPLE 1:
The following example shows how to alter all VMs to start with their ESX Host:

```
Get-VM | Get-VMStartPolicy | Set-VMStartPolicy -StartAction
PowerOn
```

EXAMPLE 2:
The following example shows how to alter all VMs to perform a guest shutdown when the host is being shutdown:

```
Get-VM | Get-VMStartPolicy | Set-VMStartPolicy -StopAction
GuestShutdown
```

EXAMPLE 3:
To view all current start policy settings for each VM:

```
Get-VM | Get-VMStartPolicy
```

Settings configured on the Virtual Machine Startup and Shutdown screen are host specific. If a VM is migrated to another host the settings will not follow the VM and it will revert to manual startup.

Creating Template VMs

Once you have begun to deploy VMs you may find it useful to start with the same base VMs to reduce the setup of the guest OS and other configuration and software options that are common to your VMs. If you have deployed vCenter server, it has functionality included to help manage your VMs and to be able to create customizations to your VMs that can be stored for repeated use. You can also manually copy a VM on a standalone vSphere host should you not be using vCenter.

When using vCenter server

1. Select the VM that you wish to convert to a VM and power it off.

2. Right click on the VM and select Convert to Template. After the process is completed, the VM will disappear from the Hosts and Cluster inventory list, but will be visible if you select the Virtual Machines tab.

PowerCLI Example

The following shows how to convert an existing VM to a template:

```
Cmdlets
Get-VM
Get-View

Related Cmdlets
Set-VM
Move-VM
New-VM
Remove-VM
Get-VIObjectByVIView

EXAMPLE 1:
Convert an existing virtual machine called PROD1 to a
template:

$ToBeTemplate = Get-VM "PROD1" | Get-View
$ToBeTemplate.MarkAsTemplate()
```

The VM will now be a template and you will be able to deploy new VMs from it. When creating a VM it's a good idea to use DHCP within the template and you can then assign a static IP address to any VMs that you deploy from that template. Windows VMs to be converted to a template can also be left in a workgroup and not joined to a domain.

If you'd like to keep a copy of your template VM running, you can also choose the Clone to Template option for the VM.

1. Right click on the VM and select the Clone to Template option. The VM can be running for this operation.

2. You will then need to assign a name to the template and select its inventory location.

3. Select the Datastore to use to store for template and then click Next.

4. On the Disk Format screen you can choose between leaving the disk format the same as the source, going with thin provisioned or using thick format. Select the format you desire and click Next and then Finish to start the clone process.

If you have added a host to vCenter Server and it contains templates, you can add those to the inventory.

1. Right click on the datastore containing the template and select Browse Datastore.

2. Find the template's VMTX file, right click and select "Add to Inventory".

3. Complete the wizard and you will then be able to view the template VM on the Virtual Machines tabs.

Once you have created your templates, you will be ready to deploy new VMs from them.

1. In the vSphere client select the Virtual Machines tab to view the templates you have available.

2. Right click on a template and select the "Deploy Virtual Machine from this Template …" option. You will notice that you also have the option to convert the template back to a VM (should you need to power it on and make updates to it) and that you can simply clone the template as well. Cloning the template makes an exact copy of the template where as the deploy VM option uses the Guest Customization wizard to customize the VM to your requirements.

3. In the Deploy Template wizard you will select the name and location for your VM and then click Next to select the host or cluster that the VM will run on.

4. The wizard will also ask for the datastore and disk format to use.

5. The next portion of the Deploy Template wizard will be the Guest Customization settings. You can choose not to customize, customize the VM using the Customization Wizard or use an existing customization specification that you've saved in the past.

6. If you select to use the Guest Customization wizard, you will be able to set the host name and domain, time zone, network IP settings, and DNS configuration. If you've added Sysprep tools to your vCenter server you will be able to set the domain, administrator password, product key and other items for Windows 2000, 2003, XP and Vista. Guest Customization is not available for all guest OSes.

7. If you wish to reuse the customization specification that you've created, you can assign a name and description to it and save it on the Save Specification screen.

8. Click Finish on the Ready to Complete screen to complete the Guest Customization wizard. You will be returned to the Deploy Template wizard where you can press finish to start the deployment process or you can select the options "Power on this virtual machine after creation" or "Edit virtual hardware (Experimental)" to add or change the hardware configuration of the VM to be deployed.

Cloning a VM without vCenter

If you don't utilize vCenter Server it is still possible to create "templates" and deploy new VMs from those templates in a more manual fashion. You will begin the process by creating a VM and configuring the guest OS to your specifications. You can add Microsoft's Sysprep or NewSID to the VM if you plan to clone Windows VMs. Once you have created the template you will want to power the VM down. To create a clone of the VM follow these steps.

1. Create a new VM with the hardware specifications that you desire, with the exception of the virtual hard disk. That can be created with a minimal size.

2. Right click on the VM in the vSphere Client and select Edit Settings ...

3. Select the virtual hard disk and click Remove. Check the option to "Remove from virtual machine and delete files from disk".

4. Click OK to commit the change.

5. You will then want to copy the virtual disk file of the template VM to the folder where your new VM resides. You will do this with the vmkfstools command which can be accessed at the console of your vSphere host or is included as part of the vCLI. The command will be run with the –i option and will look like this.

   vmkfstools –i /vmfs/volumes/<datastore name>/<source folder>/source.vmdk /vmfs/volumes/<datastore name>/<destination folder>/destination.vmdk

6. Once the VMDK file has been copied, right click on the VM again and select Edit Settings …

7. Click on Add on the Hardware tab and then select Hard Disk on the Add Hardware wizard screen.

8. On the Select a Disk screen you will choose the option "Use an existing virtual disk". On the next screen you will be able to browse to the VMDK copy that you created. Complete the Add Hardware wizard and click OK on the Virtual Machines Properties screen to commit the change.

9. Power on the VM and make any post cloning changes to the guest OS. If you used Sysprep a new SID will be created when the mini setup wizard runs.

 When running Sysprep the level of automation depends on how you set up the sysprep.inf. For a complete guide, go to:
http://support.microsoft.com/default.aspx?scid=kb;en-us;298491.

Adding VMs to Inventory on a New Host

There may be times when you find it necessary to add a number of VMs into the inventory of a vSphere host. This may occur after you have had to reinstall vSphere, after moving storage to a new host after a server failure, or after you've made a copy of a LUN for testing or disaster recovery. In any of these cases, the configuration and virtual hard drives for the VMs will still be on the datastore and it will only be a matter of adding the VMs to the inventory of the vSphere host.

On your new host you will follow this procedure.

1. In the vSphere Client, select the datastore that has the VM's files and select browse.

2. Find the VMX file for the VM, right click and select Add to Inventory. Complete the wizard and the VM will then be registered on the host.

3. You can also select Search tab of the Datastore Browser window. Then select to search for Virtual Machines and click on Search Now. A list of VMX files for that datastore will be displayed. Right click on the VMs you want to register and select the Add to Inventory option. You will only be able to register one VM at a time.

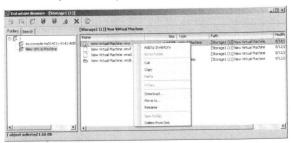

You can also perform this task at the console or with the vCLI using the vmware-cmd command. You will run the command with the following format to register a VM.

```
vmware-cmd -s o register /vmfs/volumes/<datastore
name>/<folder name>/<VM name>.vmx.
```

After you have registered your VMs, you may want to check the settings for each one. If the networking setup does not use the same VM portgroup names as the old host did, then you will need to update the virtual NICs for the VMs to reflect the new Network Label.

1. Right click on the VM in the vSphere client and select Edit Settings …

2. Select the network adapter devices and ensure that the Network Label is not blank. The summary column for the virtual NIC will display the old VM port group name, but if that port group does not exist on the new host then you will not be able to power the VM on.

You may want to consider using High Availability clusters in vCenter for VM recovery to another host. HA services will remove all the manual steps in this process and will be initiated right at the time of failure. Re-registering and firing up a large number of VMs can take time, but HA clusters can recover 20 VMs in about 5 minutes.

PowerCLI Example

The following example shows how PowerCLI can be used to register a virtual machine onto a host:

Cmdlets
```
Get-VMHost
Get-ResourcePool
Get-View
Get-DataCenter
Get-Folder
```

Related Cmdlets
```
Remove-VMHost
Move-VMHost
Set-VMHost
Add-VMHost
Get-VIObjectByVIView
New-ResourcePool
Remove-ResourcePool
Set-ResourcePool
Move-ResourcePool
Move-Datacenter
New-Datacenter
Remove-Datacenter
Set-Datacenter
New-Folder
Remove-Folder
Set-Folder
Move-Folder
```

EXAMPLE 1:
Registers PROD1 from the SAN001 datastore onto a host called MyHost in the MyDataCenter DataCenter:

```
Get-VM PROD1 | Set-VM -MemoryMB (256GB / 1MB)

$Datacenter = "MyDataCenter"
$ESXHost = "MyESXHost.mydomain.com"

$ResourcePool = Get-VMHost $ESXHost | Get-ResourcePool | Get-View
$vmFolder = Get-View (Get-Datacenter -Name $Datacenter | Get-Folder -Name "vm").id
$vmFolder.RegisterVM_Task("[SAN001] PROD1\PROD1.vmx", "PROD1", $false, $ResourcePool.MoRef, $null)
```

EXAMPLE 2:
List all VMs and their current VMX Location:

```
$Information = @()
```

```
Foreach ($VM in (Get-VM | Sort Name | Get-View)){
        $MyDetails = "" | Select-Object VMName,VMXLocation
        $MyDetails.VMName = $VM.Name
        $MyDetails.VMXLocation = $VM.Config.Files.VmPathName
        $Information += $MyDetails
}
$Information
```

Virtual Machine Resource Settings

Shares, Reservation and Limits

The use of shares, reservations and limits allow you to control CPU, memory and disk resources for a VM. These settings can have a significant impact on the performance of both the VM and host so some planning should be taken before changing these settings.

The misuse of these tools when badly understood can have detrimental effects on your environment.

Shares are a method to allocate resources during periods of contention. The shares that a VM has are relative to all the VMs running on that host or within a resource pool. When changing shares, you can raise or lower the priority of a VM for periods during which a CPU, memory or disk resource becomes limited. As you add VMs to a host or resources pool, the number of total shares increases, but the percentage of total shares that an individual VM has decreases. If you have 2 VMs on a host, one with 1000 CPU shares and the other with 500 CPU shares, during periods of CPU contention the VM with 1000 shares will receive twice the priority for CPU resources.

It is important to understand that the total share count is relative to the number of VMs on a host or in a resource pool. If you have a host with two VMs, each with 1000 shares, then there will be 2000 shares in total, and each VM would get 50% of the resource during a time of contention. If you have 10 VMs, each with 1000 shares, then there would be a total of 10,000 shares and a specific VM would get 10% of a resource. If you were to change that VM's share count to 3000, then there would now be 12,000 shares and the VM would get 25% of the resource. Note that shares only come into account when a resource is under contention. If that is not the case, then shares are ignored and a VM can use as much of a resource as it requires.

Reservations and limits are always applied to a VM. If a reservation cannot be met when you try to power on a VM, then it will not be started. Likewise, a VM will never exceed a limit when it is running. Setting a reservation allocates a minimum value of a resource that a VM will be guaranteed. That amount of a resource will always be reserved for a VM even if it is not using the full extent of its reservation. A limit is a maximum amount of a resource that a VM can use. The VM can never exceed that limit even if the host has an unallocated amount of that resource. Over allocating reservations can prevent VMs from being able to start. If you have 8 VMs, each with a 1 GHz CPU reservation, on a host with 6 GHz of CPU capacity for VMs, you will only be able to run 6 VMs at a time as the 7th will fail admission control when you attempt to power it on. Limiting a resource can have the opposite impact. If you set the limit too low, a VM may be starved for resources even though the host has plenty of free resources to offer the VM. If you set a VM CPU limit to 1 GHz, the virtual CPU in the guest will never exceed 1 GHz even if the host has available CPU capacity.

Setting Shares, Reservations and Limits on VMs

Shares, reservations and limits are set on the properties screen for a VM. By default all VMs will have shares set to Normal, Reservations set to 0 and Limit set to Unlimited. For CPU and Memory, you can set shares, reservations and limits. For Disk you can only set a value for shares.

1. In the vSphere Client, select the VM and then right click and select Edit Settings …

2. Select the Resources tab and then either Memory, Disk or CPU.

3. To change Shares, you can select between Low, Normal, High or Custom. If you select Custom you can also manually specify a value of shares to assign to the VM.

4. For Reservations you can either use the slide or manually enter a value to set the reservation in MHz or MB for the CPU and Memory options.

5. For Limit, uncheck the Unlimited option and the set the value for the Limit.

6. Click OK to save the changes that you have made.

Editing the VM will make changes similar to the below in the configuration (VMX) file for the VM.

```
sched.scsi0:0.shares = "low"
sched.cpu.min = "1000"
sched.cpu.max = "2000"
sched.cpu.units = "mhz"
sched.cpu.shares = "low"
sched.mem.minsize = "900"
sched.mem.max = "1312"
sched.mem.shares = "high"
```

In this example, Disk shares have been set too low. CPU shares have been set to low, but the VM has a reservation of 1000 MHz and a limit of 2000 MHz. The VM has a memory reservation of 900 MB, limit of 1312 MB and memory shares set to high.

Setting Shares, Reservations and Limits on Resource Pools

Shares, reservations and limits can also be applied to resource pools. The settings will then apply to the collective sum of resources that VMs within the resource pool will use.

1. In the vSphere Client, select a host or cluster, right click and select New Resource Pool …

2. Enter a name for the resource pool.

3. Configure the CPU and memory settings. There is no option to set disk shares. CPU and memory settings will apply to all child resource pools and VMs regardless of the count of those objects. If you select a CPU limit of 20 GHz, then the combined CPU usage of all VMs in that resource pool cannot exceed that limit.

4. You can also disable the Expandable Reservation option. An Expandable Reservation allows a resource pool to borrow reservation capacity from a parent resource pool, should the combined reservation of running VMs in the resource pool exceed the limit set on the resource pool. If you are uncertain on how reservations will be set on VMs in the resource pool, then it is best to uncheck this option to protect resources for other pools or VMs on the host or cluster.

Understanding How Share Values are Calculated

As mentioned above, shares dictate the relative importance of a VM's access to host resources under times of contention. A VM with twice the share count as another will be able to consume double of a resource. Shares are set to values of Low, Normal and High which corresponds to a ratio of 1:2:4. You can also choose Custom and specify the share count. The actual values for CPU and memory are in part based on the resources assigned to a VM. For CPU shares, a Low setting will grant 500 share per vCPU, 1000 shares per vCPU for Normal and 2000 shares per vCPU for High. For memory shares, a VM will get 5 shares per MB at the Low setting, 10 shares per MB at Normal and 20 shares per MB at the High setting.

In the case of a host with 4 processor cores and 5 VMs, if 4 VMs have a setting of Normal for CPU and one vCPU, they will have 1000 CPU shares each. If the 5th VM has 4 vCPUs and a share setting of Normal, the VM will have a CPU share count of 4000.

Advanced CPU Settings – Hyperthreaded Core Sharing and CPU Affinity

The Advanced CPU option on the Resources tab allows you to configure low level settings that control the scheduling of VM processing on physical CPU cores and hyperthreads. This option will not be available when the VM is running in a DRS cluster or when the VM is on a host with a single CPU core and no hypertheading.

Hyperthreading is a CPU feature which allows a single processor to run 2 independent threads at the same time. Hyperthreading delivers thread-level parallelism on each processor resulting in more efficient use of processor resources—higher processing throughput—and improved performance on the multi-threaded software of today and tomorrow. The Hyperthreaded Core Sharing option allows you to control how a VM should share a physical processor core if the host has hyperthreading enabled.

1. In the vSphere Client right click on the VM and select Edit Settings …

2. Select the Resources tab and then choose the Advanced CPU option.

3. You can choose between the following Hyperthreaded Core Sharing options.

    a. Any – the default option in which the virtual CPU of the VM will share a physical CPU core with virtual CPUs from the same VM or other VMs.

    b. None – the virtual CPUs of the VM will not share a physical core with any other virtual CPUs. In this case the other logical CPU of the physical core would be placed in a halted state.

    c. Internal – the virtual CPUs of a VM will not share the physical core with virtual CPUs from other VMs, but will share with virtual CPUs from the same VM.

CPU affinity is a feature that allows you to control which CPU cores a VM will execute on. The default setting for all VMs is No Affinity, which leaves the vSphere host free to schedule threads for the VM on any available CPU. When dealing with CPU affinity, a CPU is a logical processor or a host with hyperthreading, or a CPU core on a host with no hyperthreading. When you set CPU affinity for a VM, all the guest OS CPU threads will execute on the specified host CPUs as well as other threads (known as worlds) that are required to host the VM. This would include VM threads for emulating the VM's devices like the display, keyboard or mouse.

The default setting of No Affinity is the best option to select for most VM workloads, but in some cases you may need to set CPU affinity. This may occur if the VM is particularly CPU bound or has a licensing restriction requiring the use of a specific CPU count. To modify the VM's CPU affinity

1. In the vSphere Client right click on the VM and select Edit Settings …

2. Select the Resources tab and then choose the Advanced CPU option.

3. In the Scheduling Affinity field enter the CPUs that the VM should execute on. You can use '-' to indicate a range of CPUs or ',' to separate values. Entering 1-3, 6 would allow the VM and its related threads to execute on CPU 1, 2 ,3 and 6. Click on OK to commit your change.

4. To remove affinity settings clear the string and then click on OK.

When enabling CPU affinity for VMs, you must select at least as many processors as a VM has virtual processors allocated to it. For a dual processor VM you need to specify at least 2 CPUs in the Scheduling Affinity field. However, that could result in performance issues for the VM if the host is not able to schedule all the VM's virtual CPUs along with any related helper threads for the VM. Thus for best performance, you should allocate an additional CPU when setting CPU affinity. For a four virtual CPU VM you should assign 5 CPUs in the Scheduling Affinity field.

When a VM CPU affinity is modified, the configuration file for the VM will be updated with the following line:

sched.cpu.affinity = "value" where value is the CPUs assigned to the VM. Multiple CPUs are separated by commas and if No Affinity is set then the value will be "all".

As mentioned CPU affinity should be avoided if possible as it can create performance issues not limited to

1. CPU affinity can hinder vSphere's internal scheduler to optimally load balance CPU requests across all the host's CPUs

2. The NUMA scheduler may not be able to manage the VM that is assigned to specific CPUs with CPU affinity

3. CPU affinity can affect vSphere's ability to schedule VMs on hosts with multicore or hyperthreaded processors.

 Setting a virtual machine's CPU affinity is not allowed when the VM resides in a VMware DRS cluster. CPU affinity settings will also be cleared when a virtual machine is migrated to a new ESX host. Thus setting CPU affinity only has value when a VM will always execute on a single host.

PowerCLI Example

The following example shows how PowerCLI can be used to alter Shares, Reservations and Limits and also set and report on some of the other advanced CPU configuration options:

```
Cmdlets
Get-VM
Get-View
Get-VMResouceConfiguration
```

```
Related Cmdlets
Remove-VM
New-VM
Set-VM
Move-VM
Start-VM
Stop-VM
Suspend-VMGet-VIObjectByVIView
Set-VMResourceConfiguration
```

EXAMPLE 1:
List all Shares, Reservations and Limits for each VM.

```
Get-VM | Get-VMResourceConfiguration
```

EXAMPLE 2:
Set the Memory Limit to Unlimited for each VM which has a memory limit currently not set to Unlimited.

```
Get-VM | Get-VMResourceConfiguration | Where-Object
{$_.MemLimitMB -ne '-1'} | Set-VMResourceConfiguration -
MemLimitMB $null
```

EXAMPLE 3:
Show CPU Affinity settings for all VMs.

Managing VMs at the Console

While most of your configuration and management of VMs will be done in the vSphere Client, it is possible to perform certain functions in the console of your vSphere host.

Find the Configuration (VMX) File for a VM

If you are at the console of your vSphere host and need to find the VMX file for a specific VM, you can either search through the datastores or use the PS command to find your VM. Run the ps command as shown below adding part or the entire name for the VM.

```
ps -ef|grep -i [name or partial name]
```

In the below example, a VM called Nostalgia is being sought.

```
ps -ef|grep Nos
```

```
root 11764 1 0 21:07 ?  00:00:05
/usr/lib/vmware/bin/vmkload_app --sched.group=host/user
/usr/lib/vmware/bin/vmware-vmx -ssched.group=host/user -#
name=VMware
ESX;version=4.0.0;buildnumber=171294;licensename=VMware ESX
Server;licenseversion=4.0 build-171294; -@
pipe=/tmp/vmhsdaemon-0/vmx5b8af25c1ff961b0;
/vmfs/volumes/4a535e7d-1b11a4d5-ad10-
000c290e694b/Nostalgia/Nostalgia.vmx
root 13851 13688 0 21:23 pts/0  00:00:00 grep Nos
```

The output from the command shows the vmkload_app executing and if you follow that line you come to the important section of the return:

```
/vmfs/volumes/4a535e7d-1b11a4d5-ad10-
000c290e694b/Nostalgia/Nostalgia.vmx
```

If you use a partial name and get back multiple entries you may have to sort through them, but this is way more efficient than just browsing around the VMFS volumes.

PowerCLI Example

The following example shows how PowerCLI can be used to list all virtual machines and their VMX file location:

```
Cmdlets
Get-VM
Get-View

Related Cmdlets
Remove-VM
New-VM
Set-VM
Move-VM
Start-VM
Stop-VM
Suspend-VM
Get-VIObjectByVIView

EXAMPLE 1:
List all VMs and their current VMX Location:

$Information = @()
Foreach ($VM in (Get-VM | Sort Name | Get-View)){
       $MyDetails = "" | Select-Object VMName,VMXLocation
```

```
        $MyDetails.VMName = $VM.Name
        $MyDetails.VMXLocation = $VM.Config.Files.VmPathName
        $Information += $MyDetails
}
$Information
```

Shutdown all VMs on a Host

At some point you may need to shutdown all VMs on your host and you
won't want to do this via the vSphere Client or by running vmware-cmd
for each individual VM. To shutdown all VMs on the host run the
below command at the console.

```
vmware-cmd -l | xargs -i vmware-cmd {} stop soft
```

This command will list all the registered VMs on the host on which it is
executed and will pass a shutdown to VMs. The command assumes all
the VMs are already powered on and does not check their state, so if
there are any VMs that are registered but not powered on, the command
may return some errors. This command syntax does require VMware
Tools to be installed to be able to perform a soft shutdown of the guest
OS.

PowerCLI Example

The following example shows how PowerCLI can be used to shutdown
both VMs and ESX hosts:

Cmdlets
```
Get-VMHost
Get-ResourcePool
Get-View
Get-DataCenter
Get-Folder
```

Related Cmdlets
```
Remove-VMHost
Move-VMHost
Set-VMHost
Add-VMHost
New-ResourcePool
Remove-ResourcePool
Set-ResourcePool
Move-ResourcePool
Get-VIObjectByVIView
Move-Datacenter
New-Datacenter
Remove-Datacenter
Set-Datacenter
New-Folder
Remove-Folder
Set-Folder
Move-Folder
```

EXAMPLE 1:
```
Shutdown all guests currently powered on which are being
hosted by "HOST01.mydomain.com" and then put the host into
maintenance mode and shutdown the host:
```

```
$ESXHost = "HOST01.mydomain.com"

Get-VMHost $ESXHost | Get-VM | where {$_.PowerState -ne
"PoweredOff"} | Shutdown-VmGuest
(Get-VMHost $ESXHost | Get-View).EnterMaintenanceMode_Task(-1,
$TRUE)
((Get-VMHost $ESXHost | Get-View).ID).ShutdownHost_Task($TRUE)
```

Kill an Unresponsive VM

From time to time you will encounter a VM that seems to be hung.
Attempting to power down the VM with the vSphere Client will not
work and you may think you have to reboot the host. Before a reboot of
the host, it is worthwhile to attempt to kill the VM process at the
console.

The first command to try is vmware-cmd. In the example above the
"stop soft" option was tried which will attempt to gracefully shutdown
the guest OS. It is also possible to use the "stop hard" option as shown
below.

```
vmware-cmd /vmfs/volumes/Storage1/Nostalgia/Nostalgia.vmx stop
hard
```

If the above command is not successful, then a second method to
terminate the VM is to kill the process ID for the VM. The first step to
this is to determine the process ID with the ps command. With piping
of the output into grep it is possible to filter ps output to just show
process information for a specific VM.

```
ps -ef|grep Nostalgia
root 11764 1 0 21:07 ?   00:00:05
/usr/lib/vmware/bin/vmkload_app --sched.group=host/user
/usr/lib/vmware/bin/vmware-vmx -ssched.group=host/user -#
name=VMware
ESX;version=4.0.0;buildnumber=171294;licensename=VMware ESX
Server;licenseversion=4.0 build-171294; -@
pipe=/tmp/vmhsdaemon-0/vmx5b8af25c1ff961b0;
/vmfs/volumes/4a535e7d-1b11a4d5-ad10-
000c290e694b/Nostalgia/Nostalgia.vmx
root 13851 13688 0 21:23 pts/0  00:00:00 grep Nos
```

The process ID (PID) is the first number (11764 in the sample above)
to be returned by the command. Once you have the PID you can use
the kill command to terminate that PID.

```
kill 11764   (Where 11764 is the PID - i.e. kill <PID>)
```

After running the kill command wait for about 30 seconds to see if the
VM has been terminated. If the VM has not terminated, then rerun the
command with the -9 switch which will attempt a forcible termination
of the process as shown below. This should be a last resort.

```
Kill -9 11764
```

Configuring a Static MAC Address for a VM

When a VM is created vSphere will automatically generate a MAC address for the VM based on VMware's Organizational Unit Identifier, the SMBIOS UUID of the physical server, and a hash based on the name of the VM. Once created the MAC address of the VM will not change unless the location of the VM is changed, for example to a different path on the same host.

In some cases you may have a VM for which you want to manually set a MAC address and ensure that the address does not change over the life of the VM. It may be that you have an application that is licensed based on the MAC address of the VM or you may want to manually set the MAC address to better manage DHCP IP reservations.

To configure a static MAC address for the VM you will need to edit the properties for the VM.

1.   Ensure that the VM is powered down.

2.   In the vSphere Client, right click on the VM and select Edit Settings ...

3.   Select the network adapter device on the Hardware tab. The default MAC address option will be set to automatic and the MAC address for the VM will be displayed. A MAC address starting with 00:0C:29 will have been automatically generated by the vSphere host. An automatically generated MAC address starting with 00:50:56 will reflect that the VM was created by vCenter server.

4.   Choose the Manual option and then enter a MAC address in the range of 00:50:56:00:00:00 and 00:50:56:FF:FF:FF. A MAC address outside of that range will generate an error message.

5.   Click OK on the Virtual Machine Properties screen to save your change.

When you make this change in the vSphere client, two changes will be made to the configuration (VMX) file for the VM. First the entry

```
ethernet0.addressType = "vpx"
```

will be changed to the following

```
ethernet0.addressType = "static"
```

The below line will be added to the VMX file:

```
ethernet0.address = "00:50:56:AA:BB:CC"
```

Where AA:BB:CC is a range of address between 00:00:00 and 3F:FF:FF.

If you are using vCenter to manage your virtual machines and you want to manually edit the VMX, you will need to remove the virtual machine from vCenter before you edit the VMX file or your changes will not be saved. You can add the virtual machine back into your inventory by browsing the datastore to the virtual machine configuration file, right-clicking on the VMX file and selecting Add to Inventory.

In some cases you might have to set a MAC address that is outside of the range that is allowed by VMware. Such a case may be when you migrate a physical server to a VM and you need to retain the MAC address of the physical host. In such a case, you will have to set the MAC address at the OS level for the VM. For a Windows VM

1. Power on the VM and login.

2. Go to Control Panel \ Network Connections, right click on the network adapter and select Properties.

3. Click on the Configure option to update the network adapter.

4. On the Properties screen for the network adapter, select the Advanced tab. Then select the NetworkAddress value and set the MAC address. The MAC address should be entered as a twelve digit hex number (001CBF464410). Click OK to save your change.

On a Linux system you can run the following commands:

```
ifconfig eth0 down
ifconfig eth0 hw ether 00:1C:BF:46:44:10
ifconfig eth0 up
```

PowerCLI Example

The following example shows how PowerCLI can be used to report on the VM NIC configuration:

```
Cmdlets
Get-VM
Get-View

Related Cmdlets
Remove-VM
New-VM
Set-VM
Move-VM
Start-VM
```

```
Stop-VM
Suspend-VM
Get-VIObjectByVIView
```

EXAMPLE 1:
Display the NIC and MAC information for each VM:

```
$Information = @()
Get-VM | Get-View | ForEach-Object {
  $VM = $_
          $_.Config.Hardware.Device | Where-Object
{"VirtualPCNet32","VirtualE1000","VirtualVxmNet" -contains
$_.gettype().Name} | ForEach-Object {
                   $MyDetails = "" | Select VMname, Nictype,
MAC, MACtype
                   $MyDetails.VMname = $VM.Name
                   $MyDetails.Nictype = $_.gettype().Name
                   $MyDetails.MAC = $_.MacAddress
                   $MyDetails.MACtype = $_.AddressType
                   $Information += $MyDetails
          }
}
$Information
```

Resizing a Virtual Machine Disk File (VMDK)

When you create a VM, you will assign a virtual hard disk for the VM which the guest OS will use for system and data storage. At times you will find that you have to expand the size of the VM's storage to accommodate growth in the VM. It is possible to assign additional virtual disks to the VM, but sometimes it is easiest to just expand the VMDK that was initially created with the VM. The process for this involves first expanding the VMDK for the virtual disk to the desired size and then expanding the partitions of the guest OS.

With vSphere's Hot Extend, you can complete this procedure while the VM is powered on. For Hot Extend the disk must be in persistent mode and not have any snapshots and you must also have the vSphere host licensed at the Standard level or higher. To expand the virtual disk for the VM

1.   In the vSphere Client, right click on the VM and select Edit Settings ...

2.   Select the virtual hard disk to expand and then enter the final size that you want the virtual hard disk to be.

3.   Click OK to commit the change.

You can also expand a virtual hard disk at the console or with the vCLI using the vmkfstools command. The command is executed with the –X switch as shown in the below example.

```
vmkfstools -X 30G filename.vmdk
```

In this example, the value of 30G is the final size of the virtual disk. If you were expanding a virtual disk from 10 to 30 GB, you would use –X 30G and not –X 20G.

Once you have expanded the VMDK for the VM, you will have to update the guest OS to use the new space. You can create a new partition and then configure the guest OS to use the space. But in some cases you will want to expand the original partitions. For a system partition you will typically boot from a utility CD and then run a disk partitioning software package to expand the partition.

Using GParted

GParted is the GNOME partition editor for creating, deleting and reorganizing disk partitions. It will work with many file systems including NTFS, fat16/32 and ext3. It is available in a Live CD format, which you can use to boot your VM with -
http://gparted.sourceforge.net/download.php.

1. Ensure that your VM is powered down.

2. In the vSphere client, right click on the VM and select Edit Settings ...

3. Select the CD/DVD drive virtual device and then configure the Device Type. If you have copied the Live CD ISO image to your host's datastore, select the Datastore ISO File option and then browse to the file. Make sure the check the "Connect at power on" option for the CD/DVD device.

4. Power on the VM and in the console for the VM press ESC to access the Boot Menu. Select CD-ROM Drive to proceed to boot with the GParted Live CD.

5. When you are booting the GParted CD, you will be prompted with a number of boot up questions. Accepting the default choices will be sufficient.

6. Once GParted has started you should be able to see the hard disk for the VM. Select the partition you want to resize.

7. Then select Resize/Move from the Partition menu. Enter the appropriate values for Free Space Proceeding, New Size and Free Space Following and then select Resize/Move.

8. If you are satisfied with the change, select Apply All Operations from the Edit menu. You can also select Undo Last Operation or Clear All Operations from the Edit menu to discard changes you have made.

9. Once the resize operation has completed, select Quit from the GParted menu and then click Exit to reboot the VM. Once the VM has booted the guest OS, login and verify that the resize was successful.

Using Dell ExtPart

The Dell utility ExtPart provides support for online volume expansion of NTFS formatted Basic disks. It is available from this link - http://support.dell.com/support/downloads/download.aspx?c=us&cs=19&l=en&s=dhs&releaseid=R64398&formatcnt=2&fileid=83929

1. Power on the Windows VM and login at the console or via RDP.

2. Run the ExtPart utility and specify the drive and amount in MB by which to expand the partition. In the below example the VMDK had been expanded from 20 to 25 GB and the system partition for Windows was expanded by another 5120 MB.

```
extpart

ExtPart - Utility to extend basic disks (Build 1.0.4)
(c) Dell Computer Corporation 2003

Volume to extend (drive letter or mount point): c:

Current volume size : 20465 MB (21459722752 bytes)
Current partition size : 20465 MB (21459723264 bytes)

Size to expand the volume (MB): 5120

New volume size   : 25580 MB ((26822605312 bytes)
```

Migrate a Physical Server to a VM

One of the common aspects of moving to an environment in which virtualization is used is the need to migrate a physical server to a VM. There can be a number of reasons for this including the need to remove old hardware, supporting legacy applications or to test upgrades in a non-production environment. The process of converting from a physical to virtual server is referred to as P2V. The process of P2V consists of 3 steps:

Step 1: Preparation

Step 2: Conversion

Step 3: VM Cleanup

There are a number of tools available to support P2V conversion, both free and commercial. The products vary in what OSes they can convert, the ability to automate conversion and features like live cloning. The process below will use VMware Converter 3.0.3 (http://www.vmware.com/converter) and MOA (http://sanbarrow.com/moa.html). Both are free tools and will allow you to perform a cold clone of the physical server that you wish to P2V.

The Preparation steps are required to ensure that an image of the physical host is properly captured. Running chkdsk and a defragmentation on the physical server's drives can speed up the conversion process. In the Conversion step VMware Converter is used to copy an image of the physical server's hard drive to a VM hosted on your vSphere server. Lastly, the VM Cleanup step is necessary to remove aspects of the physical host that would have converted to the VM but may cause performance and operating issues.

Step 1: Preparation

1. Defrag the hard drives if needed.

2. Run check disk on the drives.

3. Note the following hard disk information from your source: partition sizes and drive letters, volume labels, errors in Event Viewer. Make note of any server utility partitions as you will not want to migrate those to your VM.

4. For the network configuration, make a note of the IP and MAC addresses used. If you are using NIC teaming you may wish to break the teams prior to the migration.

5. If you have any hardware agents running (i.e. from HP / Dell / IBM) then set those services to manual or disabled service startup.

6. Cleanup any temporary or unneeded files from the server.

7. If any system configuration changes or patches are pending, ensure that those have completed prior to the Conversion step.

8. Set any services to manual, which may not function properly after the P2V process. Configuration for these services can be corrected after the P2V VM is up and running.

9. Ensure that there is network connectivity between the physical host and your vSphere host. If that is not the case, then you may have to convert to a standalone VM stored on a file server, and then run VMware Converter again to transfer those files from the file server to your vSphere host.

10. Create the MOA bootable CD. Instructions on this can be found at http://sanbarrow.com. MOA creates a bootable Windows instance and allows you to run VMware Converter, VMware Workstation and other applications. You can even run a VM with ESXi to access VMFS datastores on a physical host for forensic or recovery purposes.

Step 2: Cloning

1. Boot the physical host with the MOA CD image

2. From the MOA GUI application, right click on the PC icon with the VMware logo and select to start VMware Converter.

3. Right click on the My Computer icon on the desktop and select Manage. Use the Disk Management module to verify that the partition layout is the same as was documented in item 3 of the Preparation step.

4. On the MOA GUI application, right click on the left icon and select the option to Kill Explorer.

5. Switch to VMware Converter and click on Import Machine.

6. For the Source Type select Physical Computer and click Next. Choose "This local machine" on the Source Login screen and then proceed to the Source Data screen.

7. On the Source Data screen you can choose which drives to import and if you want to resize the drives. If you are importing drives larger than 256 GB, ensure that you have formatted your VMFS datastore with the appropriate block size. The default block size for a datastore is 1 MB allowing VMDK files up to 256 GB. To import larger files you would need to choose either a 2 MB block size (for VMDK files of up to 512 GB in size, or 4 MB (1024 GB VMDK) or 8 MB (2TB-512B VMDK).

8. On the Destination Type screen you will choose the "VMware Infrastructure Virtual Machine" option to import the physical server directly to your vSphere host. If you don't have network connectivity, you can choose the "Other Virtual Machine" option and choose to save the export VM files to a file server. You can then copy these files to a PC that has network access to the vSphere host and then run VMware Converter to import the VM files to your host.

9.   On the Destination Login screen enter the IP or hostname for your vCenter Server or vSphere host as well as appropriate login credentials.

10. On the following screens you will be prompted for a name for the VM, folder location and host, cluster or resource pool from which you will run the P2V VM.

11. On the Datastore screen you will choose the location for your VM's files. If you click on advanced you can specific datastores for VM's configuration (VMX) file as well as for each virtual hard disk file.

12. On the Network screen you will choose the VM portgroup to connect to the new VM to. You can also specific how many NICs the VM will have.

13. On the Customization screen you will be able to enable options to install VMware Tools, customize the guest network identity or to remove System Restore checkpoints. The options will be dependent on the type of OS you are trying to import. Click on Next and the Finish on the Ready to Complete screen to begin converting the physical host to a VM.

Step 3: Clean Up

After the physical server has been imported to your vSphere host as a VM, you will want to power on the VM and check to see if the OS has been properly imported. Some of the items to review include

1.   Verify that all the partitions have the correct drive letters assigned.

2.   Install VMware Tools. After the install, verify that the virtual NIC settings are correct.

3.   Update the HAL if required especially when converting Windows from a multiprocessor system to a single vCPU VM.

4.   Uninstall any applications that are no longer required like hardware management agents.

5.   Enable application services that may have been disabled prior to the conversion.

6.   Review event logs and resolve any error messages.

7.   In Windows Device Manager, remove any hardware devices that are no longer required. Also edit the settings for the VM to delete unneeded hardware items like serial and parallel

ports that you will not be using. (To show the "ghosted" device follow the procedure in the following Microsoft KB article: http://support.microsoft.com/kb/315539.)

PowerCLI Example

The following example shows how PowerCLI can be used to list all Virtual machines and check their HAL version to ensure they are using the correct version.

Note: The account running this script will need to have appropriate security access to make WMI calls to the guest windows operating system.

```
Cmdlets
Get-VM

Related Cmdlets
Remove-VM
New-VM
Set-VM
Move-VM
Start-VM
Stop-VM
Suspend-VM

$HALInformation = @()
ForEach ($VM in (Get-VM))
{
        $MyDetails = "" | select-Object Name, HAL, NumvCPU
        $MYDetails.Name = $VM.Name
        $Hal = Get-WmiObject -ComputerName $VM.Name -Query
"SELECT * FROM Win32_PnPEntity where ClassGuid = '{4D36E966-
E325-11CE-BFC1-08002BE10318}'" | Select Name
        $MYDetails.HAL = $Hal.Name
        $MYDetails.NumvCPU = $VM.NumCPU
        $HALInformation += $MYDetails
}
$HALInformation
```

Migrating VMs to vSphere 4.0

At some point you may find that you want to migrate a VM running on ESX Server 3.5 or earlier, VMware Workstation or Server or another virtualization platform to vSphere 4.0. The process will typically involve copying the VM to the vSphere host and then updating the virtual hardware and VMware Tools.

Migrating a VM from ESX 3.5 or earlier to vSphere 4.0

Moving the VM can be easily done if both the vSphere and ESX host are managed by vCenter Server. vCenter Server is able to manage ESX version 2.5.5 and later. To migrate a VM in such a scenario

1. With the vSphere Client connected to vCenter Server, right click on the VM and select Migrate …

2. You will have the following 3 options for migration: change host, change datastore and change both host and datastore.

   a. The "Change both host and datastore" option is useful for migrating the VM from an ESX 2.5.5 host where the VM is stored on a VMFS2 datastore. In this case the vSphere host will need read access to the VMFS2 datastore as well as a new VMFS3 datastore large enough to hold the VM. If the vSphere host does not have access to the VMFS2 datastore, then you can power down the VM and start the migration again with the VM powered off.

      1. Select the "Change both host and datastore" option and click Next.

      2. On the Select Destination Screen, select the host or cluster to which the VM will be migrated to and click Next.

      3. Select a resource pool if one is configured and click Next.

      4. Choose the datastore that will hold the files for the VM. If you click on Advanced you will be able to select the datastores for each of the VM's virtual disks and the configuration file.

      5. On the Disk Format screen you can select the format to use for the virtual disk. You will have the option been keeping it the same as the source, converting to thick format or converting to thin format.

      6. Click Finish on the Ready to Complete screen to start the migration.

      7. After the migration is complete, the virtual hardware version will have updated from version 3 to 4 when migrating a VM from ESX 2.5.5. You can then upgrade VMware Tools and

optionally the virtual hardware version to 7 to take advantage of new vSphere features.

b. The "Change host" option is useful when moving the VM from an ESX 3.5 host to vSphere 4.0. In such a case, you may not want to migrate the storage where the VM is, but rather just the host. If VMotion is configured, you can complete this process with the VM powered on. Otherwise you will first shutdown the VM. In either case

1. Select the "Change host" option and click on Next.

2. On the next screen select the destination host or cluster and proceed to the Resource Pool screen where you will select the resource pool if applicable.

3. On the Ready to Complete screen click Finish to migrate the VM.

4. After the migration is complete you will want to upgrade VMware Tools. You can also upgrade the virtual hardware version, but once you have done that you will not be able to migrate the VM back to ESX 3.5.

If both hosts are not in the same vCenter farm, then you can consider a process similar to the cloning a VM without vCenter Server that was discussed above, or using VMware Converter in a similar method to migrating a VM from VMware Workstation or Server as discussed below. If you use VMware Converter to migrate the VM from ESX 3.5 or earlier you will

1. Power down the VM to migrate.

2. Start VMware Converter and select Convert Machine. Note that this process uses VMware Converter Standalone 4.0, while the P2V process earlier was using VMware Converter 3.0.3

3. For the Source VM, select the source type of VMware Infrastructure virtual machine and provide a hostname or IP for the ESX server or vCenter Server as well as a login and password.

4. On the next screen select the VM to migrate and then proceed to the Specify Destination tab.

5. Choose the destination type of VMware Infrastructure virtual machine and provide a hostname or IP for the ESX server or vCenter Server as well as a login and password.

6. On the following screen select the host or cluster, resource pool, VM name, datastore and virtual machine hardware version.

7. On the View/Edit Options tab you can set a number of options including the disk format (flat or thin), changing the vCPU count, changing the virtual SCSI controller and to install VMware Tools.

8. Click Next to get to the Ready to Complete tab and then click Finish to start the migration. After the migration is complete power on the VM and ensure that the migration was successful. If you hadn't selected the option, you will want to update VMware Tools and optionally upgrade the VM hardware version to 7.

If you select to use a method similar to cloning without vCenter Server, you can create a VM, edit it to remove the virtual disk and then copy the source VMDK to the new VM with the vmkfstools command as shown below. After the virtual disk is copied over, edit the VM to add the virtual disk. Then upgrade VMware Tools and optionally the virtual hardware version.

```
vmkfstools -i /vmfs/volumes/datastore1/sourcevm.vmdk
/vmfs/volumes/datastore2/targetvm/targetvm.vmdk
```

Migrating a VM from VMware Workstation/Server or other sources to vSphere 4.0

The process of migrating a VM from VMware Workstation or Server with VMware Converter is very similar to the process above to migrate from ESX to vSphere without vCenter Server. The PC on which VMware Converter is installed will require network access to the vSphere host or vCenter Server. The PC will also require file access to where the VMs are stored. VMware Converter can import a number of other different formats including VMware Consolidated Backup, Acronis True Image, Norton Ghost, and Microsoft Virtual Server.

1. Ensure that the VM you will migrate has been powered down.

2. Start VMware Converter and select Convert Machine. Note that this process uses VMware Converter Standalone 4.0,

while the P2V process earlier was using VMware Converter 3.0.3

3. For the Source VM, select the source type of VMware Workstation or other VMware virtual machine and then browse to the location of the VM's configuration (VMX) file.

4. On the Destination tab choose the destination type of VMware Infrastructure virtual machine and provide a hostname or IP for the ESX server or vCenter Server as well as a login and password.

5. On the following screen select the host or cluster, resource pool, VM name, datastore and virtual machine hardware version.

6. On the View/Edit Options tab you can set a number of options including the disk format (flat or thin), changing the vCPU count, changing the virtual SCSI controller and to install VMware Tools.

7. Click Next to get to the Ready to Complete tab and then click Finish to start the migration. After the migration is complete power on the VM and ensure that the migration was successful. If you hadn't selected the option, you will want to update VMware Tools and optionally upgrade the VM hardware version to 7.

When migrating a VM to ESX 3.5 and earlier from VMware Workstation or Server it was necessary to ensure that the virtual hard disk of the VM was changed to a SCSI disk. This could either be done manually or via tools like VMware Converter. This is no longer a concern with vSphere as IDE hard disks are now supported. However, for best performance you may still wish to convert an IDE disk to SCSI. The Configure Machine option in VMware Converter can do this.

Adding a BIOS Boot Delay to a VM

Occasionally you will have to access the BIOS of a VM to for example change the boot order. It is a common experience to have the BIOS screen pass by too quickly to allow you to press F2 to enter BIOS setup or ESC to access the boot menu. Several options have been added to make it easier to access the BIOS and BIOS setup

1. In the vSphere Client, right click on the VM and select Edit Settings …

2. Select the Options tab and then Boot Options under Advanced.

3. You can set a Power-on Boot Delay value in milliseconds. This is the amount of time that vSphere will delay in the BIOS to allow you to press F2 or other keys.

4. You can also enable the Force BIOS Setup option. If you check this, the VM will boot to the BIOS setup screen for the VM.

5. Click OK to save your changes.

The Power-on Boot Delay value will stay the same until changed, but the Force BIOS Setup option will clear after the VM has been powered on.

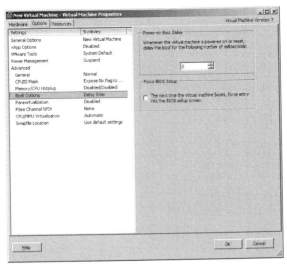

PowerCLI Example

The following example shows how PowerCLI can be used to alter the boot delay:

Cmdlets
```
Get-VM
Get-View
```

Related Cmdlets
```
Remove-VM
New-VM
Set-VM
```

```
Move-VM
Start-VM
Stop-VM
Suspend-VM
Get-VIObjectByVIView
```

EXAMPLE 1:
Set a boot delay of 5 seconds on all VMs:

```
$BootDelay = "5000"
Get-VM | ForEach-Object {
        $vm = Get-View $_.Id
        $vmConfigSpec = New-Object
VMware.Vim.VirtualMachineConfigSpec
        $vmConfigSpec.BootOptions = New-Object
VMware.Vim.VirtualMachineBootOptions
        $vmConfigSpec.BootOptions.BootDelay = $BootDelay
        $vm.ReconfigVM_Task($vmConfigSpec)
}
```

Creating a VM with a Thin Provisioned Disk

One of the new features in vSphere is support for thin provisioned virtual disks in the GUI. When you create a virtual disk for a VM and specify that it be thin provisioned, vSphere will allocate disk space to the VMDK only as the guest OS begins to require it. This is a benefit for some VMs that may require a large virtual disk when created, but will take some time to actually use the space. This feature is not recommended for high I/O VMs. Care should be taken to ensure that if the storage LUN is over allocated, that the virtual disks do not consume all available disk on the LUN. If you are using vCenter Server, you should create an alarm to alert you when the provisioned space reaches a certain threshold on the storage LUN.

1. In the vSphere Client, right click on a host, cluster or resource pool and select New Virtual Machine ...

2. On the Create a Disk screen check the option to "Allocate and commit space on demand (Thin Provisioning)".

3. Complete the New Virtual Machine.

If you are creating the virtual disk on a NFS datastore, then the option will be checked and grayed out. A message will state that the actual allocation policy will be determined by the NFS server. You can also choose the thin provisioned option when deploying a new VM from a template or when cloning an existing VM. If you have an existing VM with thick disk, you can convert those to thin using the Migrate option in vCenter Server.

1. In the vSphere Client, right click on the VM and select Migrate ...

2. Choose the migration type of Change Datastore.

3. Proceed through the wizard and on the Disk Format screen you can select the option "Thin provisioned format".

 When you browse your datastore with the vSphere Client, the full size of the virtual hard drive will be shown. So both a thick and thin VMDK of 10 GB will show as having a size of 10 GB, even though the thin VMDK may only be consumming 100 MB. Likewise at the console, running ls -lh will show the -flat.vmdk as the configured size of the virtual disk, while ls -sh will show the actual space used for the -flat.vmdk file.

Creating and Managing VM Snapshots

Snapshots are a great feature, which enables you to capture the entire state of a VM including the memory state, VM settings and disk state. This is useful for performing online hot backups of your VMs or to be able to roll back from a failed patch or system change to the guest OS. They can also be useful in a test and development environment when you need to return to the same starting point with a VM over and over.

To create snapshot

1. In the vSphere client right click on the VM and select Snapshot / Take Snapshot.

2. Enter a name for your snapshot and optionally a description.

3. You can select to take a snapshot of the VM's memory. If the VM is powered off then the option will be grayed out.

4. You can also choose the "Quiesce guest file system (Needs VMware Tools installed)" option. This option will pause running processes in the guest OS to ensure that the file system contents are in a known consistent state for the snapshot. This option requires that the VM be powered on and that VMware Tools be installed and running.

Once the create snapshot task is complete, you will be able take another snapshot, revert to the current snapshot or use Snapshot Manager select a snapshot to go to or to delete snapshots. Selecting the Create Snapshot option will create a second snapshot. This can be helpful if you are making incremental changes to the VM and want to be able to control how far back you will roll the VM back should you have a problem.

If you choose the revert to current snapshot option, the current state of memory and disk will be discarded and the VM will be restored to the state of the last snapshot taken. If you had taken 2 snapshots on a VM, the state of the VM would be reverted back to the state at the time of the 2nd snapshot.

With the Snapshot Manager screen you can have better control over the snapshots on the VM. The "You are here" icon represents the current state of the VM. To revert the VM back to a specific snapshot, select the snapshot and click on the Go to button. You can also delete snapshots. Deleting a snapshot will commit the disk snapshot data back into the parent virtual disk file and then remove the snapshot files. You can select a specific snapshot and then select Delete to only commit the changes in that snapshot into the VM, or you can select Delete All to commit all snapshot data back into the parent virtual disk file.

 Snapshots are a great feature, but can create problems in your environment. If you plan to use snapshots, make sure to allocate sufficient free disk space for the snapshot files. If you're using vCenter Server, also consider creating an alert on free disk space on your datastores as well as a VM alert on the total size in GB of snapshot files for a VM. Also keep in mind that snapshots are not intended for long term use. Leaving a snapshot on for a long time can result in a very large snapshot file which will take a very long time to commit back into the parent virtual disk file.

PowerCLI Example

The following examples show how PowerCLI can be used to manage all aspects of snapshots:

Cmdlets
```
Get-Snapshot
New-Snapshot
Remove-Snapshot
Get-VM
```

Related Cmdlets
```
Remove-VM
New-VM
Set-VM
Move-VM
Start-VM
Stop-VM
Suspend-VM
Set-Snapshot
```

EXAMPLE 1:
```
Create a new snapshot on a VM Called PROD1:
```

```
New-Snapshot -Name "General Snapshot" -VM (Get-VM "PROD1")
```

EXAMPLE 2:
Create a new snapshot on all VMs:

```
New-Snapshot -Name "All Machine Snapshot taken today" -VM
(Get-VM)
```

EXAMPLE 3:
List snapshots for all VMs:

```
Get-VM | Get-Snapshot
```

EXAMPLE 4:
List all snapshots over 14 days old:

```
Get-VM | Get-Snapshot | Where { $_.Created -lt (Get-
Date).AddDays(-14)}
```

EXAMPLE 5:
Revert the VM called PROD1 to a snapshot which is called
"First Snapshot":

```
$VM = Get-VM -Name "PROD1"
$SnapshotName = $VM | Get-Snapshot -Name "First Snapshot"
$SnapshotName | Where-Object { $_.name -like
$SnapshotName.name } | ForEach-Object { Set-VM $VM -snapshot
$SnapshotName }
```

EXAMPLE 6:
Remove all snapshots on the VM called PROD1:

```
Get-VM "PROD1" | Remove-Snapshot -confirm:$False
```

Networking

Networking in vSphere 4 is really not that complex, but the number of available options and configurations cause a lot of questions. What is a port group? Multiple port groups on a single vSwitch or single Port Group on multiple vSwitches? Specific NIC teaming per Port Group? Tag on the physical switch or on the virtual switch? Rather than focusing on design questions such as these, in this section we focus a lot on configuration and the commands associated with them. Hopefully, you will dive into this section once you have figured out your design and are ready to implement it.

vSphere Networking Fundamentals

Like VI3, the foundation of virtual networking in vSphere is the vSwitch, or vNetwork Standard Switch (vSS) as they are now called. A vSwitch provides exclusive connectivity to physical NICs (i.e. a single physical NIC cannot be shared by 2 vSwitches) and also provides a container for Port Groups. Note that every used vSwitch contains at least 1 Port Group, and this is what VM's are connected to.

Port Groups are simply logical groupings of vSwitch ports, and provide exclusive connectivity for a virtual NIC (i.e. the same virtual NIC cannot belong to more than one Port Group). Port Groups have a number of characteristics than can be modified in isolation of the vSwitch or other Port Groups, such as their VLAN membership and Traffic Shaping, Security and NIC teaming policies.

Functionally, vSwitches and Port Groups in vSphere are unchanged from VI3.

What's New

vSphere 4.0 introduces a new type of virtual switch, the vNetwork Distributed Switch (vDS, but we will call it a dvSwitch). A dvSwitch is basically a virtual switch that spans across multiple ESX hosts. This effectively splits the control and data planes of a vSwitch, moving the control plane into vCenter, and (obviously) leaving the data plane on the ESX host.

You may be thinking that this makes vCenter a single point of failure, but it doesn't – a dvSwitch works somewhat like HA, in that it can operate independently of vCenter. However just like HA, you won't be able to change any properties of a dvSwitch without vCenter, such as attaching new VM's to it.

This allows for the network state of a VM to follow it across hosts during VMotion, and also means less overhead in maintaining a consistent cluster wide networking configuration - instead of having to define Port Groups on every host in the cluster, with a dvSwitch you simply define a DV Port Group, once and it is available to any VM on any host that is connected to the dvSwitch. In addition to the DV Port Groups that the VM's are attached to, a dvSwitch has Uplink Port Groups, which are attached to the physical nics of each ESX host that is a member of the dvSwitch.

DV Port Groups are essentially the same functionally as standard Port Groups. You can assign VLAN tags to them, and modify the security, traffic shaping and NIC teaming policies on them individually. There are really only 2 additional features available with a dvSwitch, which is the capability to do inbound traffic shaping (discussed in the traffic shaping policies section), and PVLANs.

PVLANs are a standard networking construct, and as the name implies are similar conceptually to VLANs. It will be difficult to describe them without taking too much of a diversion into the realm of IP networking, but I tried. A normal VLAN is a broadcast domain – any host on a VLAN can communicate with any other host on the same VLAN. PVLANs allow traffic segregation within a VLAN, essentially simplifying IP address management. For example in a DMZ, rather than carving up a standard Class C network into multiple smaller networks to isolate hosts from one another, you could leave the Class C network as-is and use PVLANs to provide network isolation between the various hosts. Whether PVLANs are useful for your virtual environment largely depends on your networking standards and your ESX deployment plans. Within the internal network, they are probably of limited use. In DMZ deployments they may be more useful, if your networking standards allow them to be used – remember that in order to use PVLANs, the adjacent physical switches must be configured to support the use of them. This is not something that a vSphere architect or administrator can do in isolation. Talk to your networking folks – they don't bite. Much.

The technology developed for the dvSwitch also laid the foundation for 3rd party virtual switches, such as Cisco's Nexus 1000V. We will not discuss the Nexus 1000V in this book. It is worth noting also that dvSwitches are only available with the Enterprise Plus license.

vNetwork Traffic Shaping Policies

A vSwitch only has the ability to shape outbound network traffic, and can do so in three ways; Average bandwidth, burst size and peak bandwidth. Inbound traffic cannot be shaped. When you think about it, this is logical – by the time a flood of inbound traffic hits the VMkernel, there is little point in shaping it enroute to the VM - it would it be too late as the flood has consumed incoming physical network bandwidth already.

Traffic shaping is done from within a virtual switch; each virtual switch has a default vSwitch port that can manage the outbound traffic for all the physical network adapters assigned to the switch. You can adjust any of the three network policies at the vSwitch or you may edit the policies for any port group that may exist in the virtual switch.

A dvSwitch actually has both egress and ingress shaping capabilities; however the traffic shaping policies only apply to the flow between the VM and the dvSwitch - not between the dvSwitch and the physical network. Note that the vSphere Client refers to the traffic shaping policies from the perspective of the dvSwitch, so ingress traffic shaping policies apply to traffic to the dvSwitch (ie **from** the VM), and egress traffic shaping policies apply to traffic from the dvSwitch (ie **to** the VM). Read that last sentence again if you need to.

Traffic shaping polices defined on the default Uplink Group apply to the dvSwitch as a whole, and just like standard vSwitches any policy defined on a DV Port Group will override what is defined in the Uplink Group.

vNetwork NIC Teaming Policies

A physical NIC that belongs to a Standard or Distributed vSwitch can be set as Active, Standby or Unused. In addition to defining the physical NIC status, several other properties are available in the NIC Teaming Policy such as Load Balancing and Network Failover Detection.

Each Port Group of a vSwitch inherits the default NIC Teaming Policy defined for the vSwitch, and this can be overridden on the Port Group level if required.

Likewise, each DV Port Group of a dvSwitch inherits the NIC Teaming Policy defined in the Uplink Group of the dvSwitch, and this can be overridden on a DV Port Group level.

Although we are not focusing on design in this book, it's worth stressing that your NIC Teaming Policy standards take the upstream network connectivity into account in addition to the host level hardware. Using an alternate Active/Standby team when sharing 2 NICs between 2 Port Groups will not help you if those 2 NICs are connected to the same upstream switch and that upstream switch fails.

Create a vSwitch via the vSphere Client

Virtual switches are configured from the vSphere Client either connected directly to the host or to vCenter, if the host is managed by a vCenter server. In both instances, highlight the host in the left pane and then on the right pane, select the Configuration tab. There will be two boxes, Hardware and Software just about center of the screen, choose Networking in the Hardware box.

Towards the top of the screen, select Add Networking and you'll be presented with a wizard that will walk you through setting up your virtual switch.

The wizard will prompt you as to what type of network the default Port Group of the vSwitch will have, which NIC/s to bind it to and what to name the default Port Group. It is not possible to give the vSwitch a custom name when creating it via the vSphere Client.

Create a vSwitch from the command line

Virtual switches are commonly created from the vSphere Client; however, using the command line can be easier and faster. The commands can also be scripted and integrated into your automated installation if you need to.

To set up a new virtual switch called vSwitch0 and bind vmnic0 and vmnic3 to it as Active, type in the following line by line at the console prompt of an ESX/ESXi host:

```
esxcfg-vswitch -a vSwitch0
esxcfg-vswitch -L vmnic0 vSwitch0
esxcfg-vswitch -L vmnic3 vSwitch0
```

All other properties (such as security, traffic shaping and NIC teaming policies) will be set to their default values. Although these settings will take effect immediately, you'll have to restart the VMware management services on your host to see the new vSwitch in vCenter.

PowerCLI Example

The following shows how PowerCLI can be used to add a vSwitch to an ESX Host:

```
Cmdlets
```

```
New-VirtualSwitch
Get-VMHost
```

Related Cmdlets
```
Get-VirtualSwitchRemove-VMHost
Move-VMHost
Set-VMHost
Add-VMHost
```

EXAMPLE 1:
Adds a new vSwitch named vSwitch02 to the host named 'MyESXHost.mydomain.com'

```
New-VirtualSwitch -VMHost (Get-VMHost -Name
"MyESXHost.mydomain.com") -Name vSwitch02
```

Modify vSwitch properties via the vSphere Client

After a vSwitch is created, you can modify it by clicking on the Properties link just above the vSwitch (not the one on the same line as the word 'Networking'). In the dialog box that appears, you can click the Network Adapters tab to modify the physical NICs that are bound to the vSwitch, or click the Edit button to modify the number of ports the vSwitch has (host reboot required in order to take effect), the vSwitch security policy, traffic shaping policy and NIC teaming policy (no reboot required for modification of these). These settings form the default for any new Port Groups created on the vSwitch.

Once created, vSwitches cannot be renamed via the vSphere Client or the command line.

Modify vSwitch properties via the command line

Modification of vSwitch properties via the standard command line tools is basically restricted to adding/removing NICs and Port Groups – you cannot set any of the policies available via the vSphere Client.

To list all vSwitches, Port Groups and dvSwitches:

```
esxcfg-vswitch -l
```

To remove vmnic3 as an uplink from existing vSwitch0:

```
esxcfg-vswitch -U vmnic3 vSwitch0
```

To add vmnic1 as an uplink to existing vSwitch0:

```
esxcfg-vswitch -L vmnic1 vSwitch0
```

PowerCLI Example

The following shows how PowerCLI can be used to add vmnic3 as an uplink to existing vSwitch2:

```
Cmdlets
Get-VirtualSwitch
Get-VMHost
Set-VirtualSwitch

Related Cmdlets
Remove-VMHost
Move-VMHost
Set-VMHost
Add-VMHost

EXAMPLE 1:

Get-VirtualSwitch -VMHost (Get-VMHost -Name
"MyESXHost.mydomain.com") -Name "vSwitch2" | Set-VirtualSwitch
-Nic "vmnic3"
```

Create a Port Group via the vSphere Client

To create a Port Group via the vSphere Client, select the host that you wish to create the Port Group on, click on the configuration tab, click "Networking" in the Hardware section then click on the "Add Networking" link in the top right corner.

The Add Network wizard will appear. Select the type of Port Group you wish to create then click Next, select the vSwitch that you wish to create the Port Group on then click Next, name the Port Group and set a VLAN ID if required then click Next, and finally click Finish.

Create a Port Group via the command line

To add a Virtual Machine Port Group "Production" to vSwitch0, type in the following at the console of the host:

```
esxcfg-vswitch -A "Production" vSwitch0
```

To add a VMkernel Port Group on vSwitch0, first create the Port Group:

```
esxcfg-vswitch -A "VMotion" vSwitch0
```

Then add a VMkernel NIC to it:

```
esxcfg-vmknic -a -i 10.0.0.1 -n 255.255.255.0 -p "VMotion"
```

If you wish to enable a Port Group for VMotion, first get the vmknic interface name by listing all VMkernel NICs and finding the target one:

```
esxcfg-vmknic -l
```

If the relevant vmknic interface was "vmk1" enable it for VMotion with:

```
vim-cmd hostsvc/VMotion/vnic_set vmk1
```

PowerCLI Example

The following shows how PowerCLI can be used to add a portgroup
named PG1 to vSwitch2 on 'MyESXHost.mydomain.com':

```
Cmdlets
Get-VirtualSwitch
Get-VMHost
New-VirtualPortGroup
```

```
Related Cmdlets
Set-VirtualSwitch
Remove-VMHost
Move-VMHost
Set-VMHost
Add-VMHost
Remove-VirtualPortGroup
Set-VirtualPortGroup
Get-VirtualPortGroup
```

```
EXAMPLE 1:
```

```
Get-VirtualSwitch -VMHost (Get-VMHost -Name
"MyESXHost.mydomain.com") -Name vSwitch2 | New-
VirtualPortGroup -Name PG1
```

```
vim-cmd hostsvc/VMotion/vnic_set vmk1
```

Modify Port Group properties via the vSphere Client

To modify Port Group properties via the vSphere Client, select the host
that you wish to modify, click on the configuration tab, click
"Networking" in the Hardware section then click on the "Properties"
link of the vSwitch that contains the Port Group you wish to modify.

A dialog box will pop up with a list of the Port Groups configured on
the vSwitch. Highlight the one you wish to modify, then click the Edit
button. You will be presented with a tabbed dialog box, where you can
modify the Port Group name, VLAN, Security Policy, Traffic Shaping
Policy and NIC Teaming policy.

Modify Port Group properties via the command line

Modification of Port Group properties via the standard command line
tools is pretty much restricted to changing the VLAN and
adding/removing NICs.

To set VLAN 13 on existing Port Group "Production" on vSwitch0:

```
esxcfg-vswitch -v 13 -p "Production" vSwitch0
```

To remove vmnic0 from existing Port Group "Production" on vSwitch0:

```
esxcfg-vswitch -N vmnic0 -p "Production" vSwitch0
```

To delete existing Port Group "VM Network" from vSwitch0:

```
esxcfg-vswitch -D "VM Network" vSwitch0
```

PowerCLI Example

The following shows how PowerCLI can be used to alter and delete Port Groups:

Cmdlets
```
Get-VirtualSwitch
Get-VMHost
New-VirtualPortGroup
```

Related Cmdlets
```
Set-VirtualSwitch
Remove-VMHost
Move-VMHost
Set-VMHost
Add-VMHost
Remove-VirtualPortGroup
Set-VirtualPortGroup
Get-VirtualPortGroup
```

EXAMPLE 1:
The following example can be used to set the Port Group ID to 13 on the Port Group PG1:

```
Get-VirtualSwitch -VMHost (Get-VMHost -Name
"MyESXHost.mydomain.com") -Name vSwitch2 | Get-
VirtualPortGroup -Name PG1 | Set-VirtualPortGroup -VLanId 13
```

EXAMPLE 2:
The following example can be used to delete the Port Group named PG1:

```
Get-VirtualSwitch -VMHost (Get-VMHost -Name
"MyESXHost.mydomain.com") -Name vSwitch2 | Get-
VirtualPortGroup -Name PG1 | Remove-VirtualPortGroup
```

Create a Distributed vSwitch via the vSphere Client

Distributed vSwitches must be created from the Networking Inventory section of the vSphere client, rather than via the Networking configuration section of an individual host. To create a dvSwitch, simply right click the datacenter object that contains the hosts / clusters you want to configure with the dvSwitch and choose "New vNetwork Distributed Switch". The wizard only has 3 steps:

1) Name the dvSwitch, and chose the number of Uplink Ports

2) Add hosts and their physical NICs. This can be done later.

3) Finally, decide whether you want a DV Port Group created automatically or not, and then click Finish.

You will now see a dvSwitch object in the inventory, containing an Uplink Group and a DV Port Group if you opted to auto-create one.

You will now need to add hosts and their physical NICs to the dvSwitch. To do so, right click the dvSwitch and choose "Add Host". The wizard presents a list of hosts that have Enterprise Plus licenses, along with the physical NICs that are available on each host.

It is recommended you have a look at the "Migrate from Standard vSwitches to a Distributed vSwitch" section of this chapter before adding any hosts to a dvSwitch.

Finally, you are presented with a confirmation dialog. Click "Finish".

Modify Distributed vSwitch properties via the vSphere Client

To modify a dvSwitch, go to the Networking Inventory section of the vSphere client, right click the relevant dvSwitch and choose "Edit Settings".

There are 3 tabs in the dvSwitch Settings dialog box. In the General view of the first tab, you can rename the dvSwitch, modify the number of uplink ports and modify the notes field of the dvSwitch. The Advanced view of the first tab exposes MTU and CDP settings. The Network Adapters tab allows you to view the NIC and dvUplink assignments for a host, however you cannot modify them here – to modify them, you need to go to the usual Networking section in the Configuration tab of the host you wish to modify. The 3rd tab, Private VLAN allows you to define PVLANs.

Modify Distributed vSwitch properties via the command line

Like Standard vSwitches, modificaton of dvSwitch properties via the standard command line tools is basically restricted to adding/removing

NICs and DV Port Groups – you cannot set any of the policies available via the vSphere Client.

To remove vmnic3 from a DVUplink on DV Port ID "777" on dvSwitch "dvSwitch":

```
esxcfg-vswitch -Q vmnic3 -V "777" dvSwitch
```

To remove a VMkernel nic from DV Port ID "666" on dvSwitch "dvSwitch":

```
esxcfg-vmknic -d -s "dvSwitch" -v "666"
```

Modify Uplink Group properties via the vSphere Client

To modify a DV Port Group, go to the Networking Inventory section of the vSphere client, right click the relevant DV Port Group and choose "Edit Settings". Whatever options you choose here will become the defaults for any DV Port Groups created on the dvSwitch.

In the General section, you can modify the Name, Description, Number of Ports and the Port Binding. The Port Binding options refer to how VM's are attached to the DV Port Group – either statically (same DV Port used across VM power states), dynamically (DV port assigned upon VM power on operation), or Ephemeral (for all intents and purposes, no binding at all).

The Policies section presents the Security, Traffic Shaping, VLAN, Teaming and Miscellaneous configuration settings all in one messy dialog. Or, you can view the available settings for each in isolation by clicking the relevant heading in the menu. That must have been one heck of an argument between the UI designers and someone in management, one can only assume that the UI designers lost.

Finally, the Advanced section contains some port specific configuration options, such as whether the DV Port Group settings will override individual dvPort settings and the dvPort naming format.

Create a DV Port Group via the vSphere Client

To create a DV Port Group, go to the Networking Inventory section of the vSphere client, right click the relevant dvSwitch and choose "New Port Group". The wizard that appears basically has a single step allowing you to configure the DV Port Group name, the number of ports and the VLAN.

Modify a DV Port Group via the vSphere Client

Although hardly any options are presented when creating a DV Port Group via the vSphere client, there are many options available for modification after the DV Port Group has been created.

To modify a DV Port Group, go to the Networking Inventory section of the vSphere client, right click the relevant DV Port Group and choose "Edit Settings". All the available options in the resulting dialog are the same as those discussed in the preceding "Modify Uplink Group properties via the vSphere client" section.

Migrate from Standard vSwitches to a Distributed vSwitch

Distributed vSwitches may not be something you want to entertain at the same time as you deploy vSphere, however all designs should be revisited periodically to ensure that the design assumptions and assertions are still valid. To that end, migrating from Standard vSwitches to Distributed vSwitches is something you might consider doing post-vSphere deployment.

Migrating from vSwitches on multiple hosts to a single dvSwitch can be a completely non-disruptive process, as long as you have redundant NIC teaming in place for all existing Port Groups or at least have the capability to reconfigure your current NIC teaming setup prior to the migration in order to ensure that you can run the existing vSwitches in parallel with the new dvSwitch until all VM's are migrated across. Of course, during the course of the migration it may be acceptable to have non-redundant physical network connectivity in order to ensure a seamless migration.

Assuming the above, you can perform a completely non-disruptive migration from standard vSwitches to a Distributed vSwitch as follows:

Before doing anything, ensure the NIC teaming configuration on the existing vSwitches and Port Groups is consistent across all hosts, and ensure that no VM's are actively using a vmnic that is also in active use by a VMkernel or Service Console Port Group. This will ensure you don't get any surprises when removing the physical NICs from the vSwitch and attaching them to the dvSwitch. Record the names of the VMkernel / Service Console vmnics somewhere if you need to. Additionally, make sure you have some level of networking redundancy for your existing VM Port Groups, to ensure a seamless migration of the VM's.

1) Create a new dvSwitch as per the previous section "Create a Distributed vSwitch via the vSphere Client". Do not add any hosts to the dvSwitch at this time.

2) Create DV Port Groups that map to the existing standard vSwitch Port Groups. Ensure that any required VLAN configuration is done correctly on the new DV Port Groups. If using a different naming convention for the DV Port Groups, it's probably not a bad idea to map the Port Groups to DV Port Groups out in a spreadsheet before proceeding.

3) It's now time to add hosts to the dvSwitch. Right click the dvSwitch and choose "Add Host". You will be presented with a list of available adapters on each host that are already in use by the existing vSwitch/es. Select all the VMkernel vmnics on one of the hosts. Resist the temptation to add any vmnics being used for Virtual Machine networking, we'll get to that later.

4) The Add Host wizard will recognize that you are migrating NICs that are already attached to standard vSwitches, and will present a dialog box allowing you to map the old Port Groups to the new. It is critically important that you have the Management or Service Console connections mapped correctly, as the wizard will migrate these connections to the new dvSwitch immediately and delete the old Port Groups from the Standard vSwitches on the host. The Virtual Machines on the other hand will remain running on the existing Standard vSwitches – you will migrate them separately a little later on.

5) You will finally be presented with a confirmation dialog. Double check that all your mappings are correct, then hit Finish. An "Update network configuration" task will be invoked.

6) You will know that you have done everything correctly if your test host still appears connected in the vSphere Client when the "Update network configuration" task completes. If that is the case, you can now go through the Add Host wizard again as many times as needed, and add the rest of the hosts and their VMkernel / Service Console vmnics. If your host appears disconnected in the vSphere Client at any time, something has gone wrong – don't migrate any more hosts and skip to the end of this section now!

7) You can now test a migration of a VM across to the new dvSwitch. First, you need to add one of the vmnics currently being used by VM's to the dvSwitch. To do this, go back to the Hosts and Cluster Inventory view, select the host you are using for testing, go to the Configuration tab and to the networking section. Click on the grey "Distributed Virtual Switch" button, then click the blue "Manage Physcial Adapaters" link. A dialog box will appear, click the "Click to Add NIC" link under the dvUplink you wish to use, and choose a standby vmnic being used for VM networking (or if you are running multiple active vmnics for your VM's, choose a single active one) and click OK.

8) Now that you have a phsycial NIC attached to the dvSwitch that you can use for VM networking, go back to the Networking Inventory view, right click on the dvSwitch as if you were going to add another host to the dvSwitch, but choose "Migrate Virtual Machine Networking" from the context menu.

9) The Migrate Virtual Machine Networking wizard will appear, allowing you to migrate VM's an entire Port Group at a time if you want to. But since this is a test, simply select a Source and Destination Network, click "Show Virtual Machines", choose a single VM and hit OK. If the migration is successful (ie you still have network connectivity to the VM after it's attached to the dvSwitch), re-run this wizard as many times as you need to in order to migrate all VM's to the dvSwitch.

10) Everything should now be working correctly with all VM's and VMkernel networks operating via the dvSwitch. You can now migrate the rest of the vmnics from the old Standard vSwitches to the new dvSwitch. Follow the procedure detailed in step 8 to do this.

11) Finally, if everything is working correctly you can remove the old vSwitches from each host.

If your migration test fails and you need to back out the change made to the test host, you will likely have lost network connectivity to your ESX host. In order to restore connectivity, log on to the console of the host and use a combination of the commands in the previous sections to remove all VMkernel NICs and vmnics from the dvSwitch then recreate your original Service Console / Management Network setup.

Setting NIC speeds and duplex

You can either set the speed and duplex using the vSphere Client or at the command line.

To do it from the vSphere Client, highlight the host you wish to modify, go to the Configuration tab, then Networking and select the properties for each virtual switch. Click on the Network Adapters tab and then the edit button. Choose the appropriate speed and duplex settings for your environment.

To do this from the command line use the esxcfg-nics command:

```
esxcfg-nics -s 1000 -d full vmnic0
```

In the example above you are setting vmnic0 to and setting its speed (-s) to 1000 and its duplex (-d) to full.

Installing additional NICs in your ESX host

Installing an additional NIC in ESX 4.0 can be done through vCenter or the Service Console.

You would first have to place the ESX host in to maintenance mode. Power down your ESX host and physically install your new NIC. Once you power on your ESX host your configuration will be done from either vCenter or the Service Console. Here's the procedure for vCenter:

1. Choose the ESX host you added the NIC to

2. Choose the Configuration tab

3. Choose networking

4. Choose a vSwitch you want to add the NIC to and select properties (or create a new one)

5. From within properties select the Network adapters tab

6. Choose add and the add adapters wizard starts

7. Select the NIC you installed

8. Choose Next

9. Choose finish at the summary page.

The Service Console procedure is straightforward:

1. Find out which "vmnic" has been added:
   ```
   esxcfg-nics -l
   ```

2. Add a vmnic to a vSwitch:

```
esxcfg-vswitch -L vmnic5 vSwitch0
```

How do I check my network speed or link status from the Service Console?

You can check your network interface's speed and duplex, log into the Service Console of the host and run:

```
esxcfg-nics -l
```

Note that the final character in this command is a lower case "L" not a 1. This will give you a return with the name, driver, links speed and duplex as follows:

```
Name PCI    Driver Link Speed  Duplex Description
vmnic0 06:07.00 e1000 Up 100Mbps Full Intel
vmnic1 07:08.00 e1000 Up 10Mbps Half Intel
```

Note we have shortened the description here for easier reading.

PowerCLI Example

The following example shows how PowerCLI can be used to report all nic speeds:

Cmdlets
Get-VMHost

Related Cmdlets
Remove-VMHost
Move-VMHost
Set-VMHost
Add-VMHost

EXAMPLE 1:
The following example lists all hosts nics and nic speeds

```
Write "Gathering VMHost objects"
$vmhosts = Get-VMHost | Sort Name | Where-Object {$_.State -eq
"Connected"} | Get-View
$Information = @()
foreach ($vmhost in $vmhosts){
        $ESXHost = $vmhost.Name
        Write "Collating information for $ESXHost"
        $networkSystem = Get-view
$vmhost.ConfigManager.NetworkSystem
        foreach($pnic in $networkSystem.NetworkConfig.Pnic){
                $pnicInfo =
$networkSystem.QueryNetworkHint($pnic.Device)
                foreach($Hint in $pnicInfo){
                        $NetworkInfo = "" | select-
Object Host, PNic, Speed
                        $NetworkInfo.Host = $vmhost.Name
                        $NetworkInfo.PNic = $Hint.Device
                        $record = 0
                        Do{
```

```
                                        If ($Hint.Device -eq
$vmhost.Config.Network.Pnic[$record].Device){

        $NetworkInfo.Speed =
$vmhost.Config.Network.Pnic[$record].LinkSpeed.SpeedMb
                                        }
                                        $record ++
                        }
                        Until ($record -eq
($vmhost.Config.Network.Pnic.Length))
                                $Information += $NetworkInfo
            }
        }
}
$Information | Sort Host, PNic
```

Troubleshooting console connectivity

Troubleshooting console connectivity is not as difficult as you would think. It does, however, need to be done from the actual console and you only need to use a few different commands. If you're like any other shop in the world, then you'll need to do your due diligence on the server before yelling at your networking team. Unless you don't like them, in which case go right ahead and start yelling.

Step 1: Check your physical connectivity

Many an enraged accusation has been caused by physical failure. Although getting physical access to a datacenter is on par with the vault of Fort Knox these days, checking the physical status of your machine and cabling should be your first port of call.

Step 2: Check connectivity from your console

    a)   Access the local console of the machine via a KVM (direct or over IP) or an out-of-band management tool like HP iLO, Dell DRAC or IBM RSA.

    b)   If using ESX, login and run ifconfig to view the information for your Service Console, make sure you have an IP address configured. If using ESXi, use the DCUI to view the management IP address of the host.

    c)   Try to ping your default gateway or another known IP. For ESXi, this can be done via the Test Management Network option of the DCUI.

    d)   Use the esxcfg-nics -l command from a shell prompt to check links status (up or down), speed and duplex settings

Step 3: Check your Virtual Switch and Service Console Configuration

a)   List your current Virtual Switches by typing in:

```
esxcfg-vswitch -l
```

Look at the output and take note to which NICs are bonded to which switches. Look to see if you have a Service Console Port Group.

b)   Next, take a look at your Service Console settings:

```
esxcfg-vmknic -l
```

Ensure IP address netmask etc looks correct.

c)   Finally, check the VMkernel route table:

```
esxcfg-route -l
```

Ensure IP address netmask etc looks correct.

Step 4: Create a temporary Service Console

If your SC has been deleted or isn't listed or is but isn't functioning, create a new Virtual Switch and bond it to a NIC that is known to be connected to the same network as the original NIC or even create a brand new one.

a)   To create a new virtual switch:

```
esxcfg-vswitch -a vSwitchX
esxcfg-vswitch -L vmnicX vSwitchX
```

b)   Create a Port Group within the vSwitch

```
esxcfg-vswitch -A "Service Console Temp" vSwitchX
```

c)   Add a new vmknic mapped to the Port Group and set the IP / Subnet Mask:

```
esxcfg-vmknic -a -i x.x.x.x -n y.y.y.y -p "Service
Console Temp"
```

Be sure to add a unique, valid IP

d)   Restart the management service:

```
service mgmt-vmware restart
```

Step 5: Reconnect to your host

a)   Ping from the new Service Console an IP from another host or a workstation.

b) If it responds, connect using the vSphere Client and go the configuration tab to check networking and if necessary, recreate your original virtual switches and Port Groups.

c) If it doesn't you may have to reboot the host.

Overview of vNetwork commands

Modifying and troubleshooting virtual switches often require you "dig in" to some different command line utilities. Initially you can reconfigure network settings and troubleshoot problems via the virtual infrastructure client (if you are not experiencing a problem with the Service Console).

In certain scenarios you may experience an outage with the Service Console's network connection or may need to move to the command for "deeper" troubleshooting. When this happens you need to troubleshoot the problem by connecting directly to the services console of the ESX host itself and will most likely need some of the following commands:

Command	Description
esxcfg-vmknic -l	Lists VMkernel network interfaces.
esxcfg-vswitch -l	Lists vSwitches and Port Groups.
esxcfg-vswif -l	Lists Service Console
exscfg-nics -l	Lists physical network adapters.
esxcfg-route -l	Lists VMkernel network routes.

Using the various options available in these commands from the Service Console of an ESX host should give you the ability to reconfigure network connectivity for the host and any virtual switches that are configured within the host.

Storage

Storage and the associated infrastructure in an ESX environment are
often the most expensive and misunderstood components in the virtual
datacenter. While there will always be a great discussion on the best
types of storage (just like the best types of servers), the reality is that
storage is what it is—namely, disk, a means of providing a secure
location to store your information. The goal is to keep it simple.
However, it is important to understand how ESX connects to and uses
available storage. Additionally, a good knowledge of the related
technologies, in addition to the configuration and management tools,
will help to ensure success.

This section starts with some storage basics such as; viewing
information about the available storage and the parameters regarding
such. From there, the text then moves on to topics like Raw Device
Mappings (RDMs), iSCSI (VMFS) and NFS volumes and even some
pointers/tips on storage arrays from different manufactures/providers.

Once we cover these items we'll look at new capabilities available with
ESX 4.0 (vSphere). This will include a review of the pluggable storage
architecture (PSA) and the benefits of this enhancement.

Viewing disk space in use

To view the available physical partition space for an ESX hosts, run the
following command from the Service Console: (assuming ESX not
ESXi, if you are using ESXi some of this information is viewable via the
"unsupported" CLI or via the RemoteCLI tools)

```
df -h (the -h provides a "human readable" format)
```

The df command will provide basic file system disk space usage for
traditional Linux volumes.

```
[root@esx10 ~]# df -h

Filesystem          Size Used Avail Use% Mounted on
/dev/sda2           4.9G 1.4G 3.2G 31% /
/dev/sda1            99M 29M 66M 31% /boot
none                132M  0 132M  0% /dev/shm
/dev/sda6           2.0G 46M 1.8G  3% /var/log
```

To view VMware File System (VMFS) volumes/datastores in addition
to the standard Linux volumes used by the ESX Service Console (COS),
use the VMware command 'vdf':

```
vdf -h
```

```
[root@esx10 ~]# vdf -h
Filesystem      Size Used Avail Use% Mounted on
/dev/sda2       4.9G 1.4G 3.2G 31% /
/dev/sda1        99M  29M  66M 31% /boot
none                      132M   0 132M  0% /dev/shm
/dev/sda6       2.0G  46M 1.8G  3% /var/log
```

Notice that the output is identical to this point. The remainder is
specific to the VMFS datastores to which this particular ESX server
has visibility. The following has been reformatted for readability.

■■

```
/vmfs/devices   265G   0 265G   0% /vmfs/devices

/vmfs/volumes/44d886b1-aa3e931b-b2b6-001143dd0857

                128G  46G  82G 36% /vmfs/volumes/storage1
```

■■

You can also use the vSphere Client to view VMFS datastores.
While attached to your vCenter server, navigate to View Menu→
Inventory→ Datastores.

Selecting a datacenter provides a view of all associated free storage
for that connected ESX hosts and the VMs contained within.

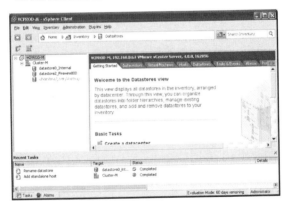

For a view of storage associated with a specific ESX host, go to the
View menu→ Inventory→ Hosts & Clusters. Expand a datacenter,
(optional - expand a cluster), and select a specific ESX host. Select the
Configuration tab and navigate to the "Storage (SCSI, SAN, and NFS)"
section under the Hardware list.

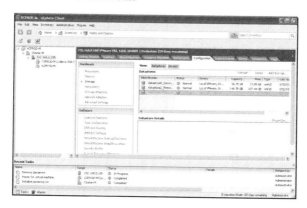

PowerCLI Example

The following shows how PowerCLI can be used to report on datastore
information

Cmdlets
Get-Datastore

Related Cmdlets
New-Datastore
Remove-Datastore
Set-Datastore

EXAMPLE 1:
Gets a list of all datastores attached to
MyESXHost.mydomain.com

Get-Datastore -VMHost (Get-VMHost "MyESXHost.mydomain.com")

Modifying local ESX partitions

Local ESX partitions can be created or modified during the initial
installation of the host server. By default, VMware will create partitions
for you. By selecting the Advanced setting during the installation
procedure, you will have the ability to edit the default volumes or create
new ones.

Once an ESX server is up and running use the 'fdisk' command from the Service Console to edit or add local partitions. This command is the same command available with most Linux distributions.

The following are the usage commands for the 'fdisk' utility:

```
Usage: fdisk [-b SSZ] [-u] DISK  - Change partition table
fdisk -l [-b SSZ] [-u] DISK      - List partition table(s)
fdisk -s PARTITION               - Show partition size(s)
blocks
fdisk -v                         - Show fdisk version
```

For a complete listing of the fdisk command available switches, enter the following command from the Service Console: man fdisk

Numerous examples of fdisk, its usage and a veritable plethora of documentation exist online. Of course, one of your best resources of information comes from Internet search tools. Use Google or another search tool to lookup fdisk.

We just want to make sure you know that you can use fdisk. The tool works best if you happen to have some unused/non-partitioned space on the host.

Try it out on a test ESX server.

Using an NFS mount

There are a couple of Console OS items and that need to be completed before you can add an NFS mount through vCenter for your ESX host. Once these are done, it is a pretty straightforward process to configure and mount anNFS export.

From the COS:

1. Log in as a root user

2. Enter "esxcfg-firewall -e nfsClient" which will enable the firewall ports 111 for UDP and 2049 for TCP

3. Enter "chkconfig --level 345 portmap on" to enable the portmap service and makes it persistent after a reboot

4. Enter "service portmap start" which starts the portmap service

5. Enter "chkconfig --level 345 netfs on" which enables the netfs service and makes it persistent after reboot

6. Enter "service netfs start" which will start the netfs service which allows multiple identical mounts

7. Enter "`chkconfig --level 345 nfs on`" to make the nfs service persistent after reboot

8. Enter "`service nfs start`" to start the nfs service

By enabling these ports and services from the COS, you are ensuring that the NFS will mount from vCenter.

The configuration from vCenter looks like this:

1. Choose a host from inventory

2. Choose the configuration tab

3. Choose Security Profile under the Software Panel

4. Choose Properties

5. Enable the NFS Client

6. Choose Storage from the Hardware Panel

7. Choose Add Storage. The Select Storage Type page displays

8. Choose Network File System

9. Type in the server name

10. Type in the folder name (A.K.A. mount point).

11. Enter a name for the datastore

12. Choose Next

13. Choose Finish

PowerCLI Example

The following shows how PowerCLI can be used to add an nfs store to multiple ESX Hosts

Cmdlets
New-Datastore

Related Cmdlets
Get-Datastore
Remove-Datastore
Set-Datastore

EXAMPLE 1:
Add the NFSStore01 NFS share to all hosts in the Non Production cluster.

```
Get-Cluster "Non Production" | Get-VMHost | New-Datastore -Nfs
-Name NFSStore01 -NFSHost nfs.mydomain.com -Path NFSStore01
```

What is a LUN and how do I create one?

Definition: A logical unit number or LUN is an address for an individual disk drive and by extension, the disk device itself. The term originated in the original SCSI protocol as a way of differentiating individual disk drives within a common SCSI target device like a disk array.

LUNs are storage volumes that are mounted by ESX hosts and are used to store virtual machine configurations and disk (.vmdk) files.

Creating a LUN is typically done by a storage engineer/administrator within your organization. The problem that often presents itself in an ESX environment is the definition of a "LUN". It can and does vary between storage manufacturers. Within ESX, a LUN is considered a block of storage or volume as it is presented to the ESX host. Most ESX administrators refer to a single VMFS volume on that block of storage as a LUN, so when conversing with a VMware Administrator you may hear "I couldn't see the LUN," "I had the storage guy zone the LUN to the hosts…," "How big are your LUNs" and basically you should know that when talking LUNs to an ESX guy, you are pretty much talking about VMFS volumes stored on SAN arrays and presented to ESX servers.

LUNs can be created on all different types of storage devices, from local SCSI- or SATA-attached storage arrays to large storage area network (SAN) devices. And, by the way, you really don't create them on the ESX side. All you do is scan for them (in the storage view of the configuration tab for a specific ESX host or a group of hosts from a vSphere vCenter Server) and format them (generally VMFS). Of course the scan and format processes are part of the Add Storage Wizard, which is a simple point-and-click tool.

For more information on creating LUNs for use in a vSphere infrastructure, see the section, 'How should I set up my LUNs on my SAN for ESX?'

How many LUNs and paths can I have?

This question is often asked as you begin to look at the amount of storage you need for all of your VMs. With ESX 4.0, the number of supported LUNs and paths to the LUNs has remained the same as compared to ESX 3.5. The total number of paths to a particular LUN has dropped from 32 to 16. Besides LUNs however, you have a number of other configuration maximums within the environment that you, as the administrator, should be aware of. In the list below we show

LUN information, the number of paths between storage and a number of additional parameters.

This information is found in VMware's Storage Compatibility guide.

http://www.vmware.com/resources/compatibility/pdf/vi_san_guide.pdf

The following system and virtual machine maximums are supported for ESX hosts:

- Maximum LUNs per system: 256 (128 during install)
- Maximum HBAs per system: 16 ports (4 quad port cards, 8 dual port cards, etc.)
- Maximum virtual HBAs per virtual machine: 4
- Maximum targets per virtual HBA: 15
- Maximum virtual disks per Windows virtual machine: 60
- Maximum virtual disks per Linux virtual machine: 60
- Maximum number of VMFS file systems per server: 256
- Maximum disk space per VMFS: 2TB-512B * # of extents
- Maximum file size per VMFS-3 file: Default max file size for VMFS 3 is 256GB (block size of 1MB). This can be configured to a block size of 8MB which will allow a 2TB-512B file.
- Maximum number of files per VMFS-3: Supports enough files to hold the maximum number of VMs per VMFS volume supported by ESX 3.0 (typically greater than 30,000 files)
- Maximum number of paths per LUN: 32
- Maximum number of targets per HBA: 15
- Minimum VMFS-3 volume size: 1.1 GB

The trick is to understand what it all means to you beyond the number of LUNs. LUN counts are simple, max 256. Path counts often are more confusing.

Let's assume you have one LUN exposed to your server. In the server you have two single-port FibreChannel HBAs connected to a simple fabric with an Active/Passive storage system like an EMC Clariion (CX 3-80). In this case you should do some simple math:

Number of LUNs * (number of HBA ports * storage processors each HBA port sees) = total number of paths.

The result is simple: 1 * (2 * 1) = 2. You have two paths out from that server. This can become a larger number in more complex systems. Now let's assume you have 56 LUNs, with two dual-port FibreChannel HBAs in each server and each port can see just one storage processor. Now the formula looks like this: 56 * (4 * 1) = 224 paths from the system.

How big should my VMFS volumes be?

This is truly a question for the ages. VMFS volumes should be as big as possible without affecting performance of the VMs or hosts. If the VMFS volumes are too small, you wind up with a large number of volumes and paths that you have to manage and that ESX has to scan as it boots. This leads to complexity and longer boot cycles. If your VMFS volumes are too large, you may affect performance on the array and therefore the VMs, or you may wind up with to many VMs on a single LUN and the amount of I/O on that LUN could drag down performance. Sizing LUNs is really a game of averages and it has as much to do with your standards for disk/file system management.

First off, a VMFS-3 volume must be at least 1.2GB. After the minimum is established, you should figure out your basic VMFS layout. General rule of thumb says no more than 32 VMs per VMFS volume. While this often works from a disk I/O standpoint, sizing becomes an issue due to the space required by the VMs.

In some cases, as with EMC Symmetrix (DMX) storage, the optimal LUN size from an array standpoint may be too small to allow 32 VMs to be stored on a single LUN. So the first question is to determine the optimal configuration for your array. When leveraging EMC storage, the optimal size for DMX is generally about 136GB per LUN, and with the CX-series storage it is often 250GB or 500GB. Check with your particular storage vendor to determine optimal size for your array. For this example we'll use the EMC CLARiiON (CX) figures.

If we are presented with options for 250GB or 500GB, we can then do some simple math. Assume that my average VM needs 20GB worth of space in my vmdk. Add to that the amount of space needed on the VMFS volume for swap, .vmx config files and maybe snap shots. This adds another, say, 5GB. That brings us up to 25GB per VM. In a 500GB LUN you would most likely get 18 or 19 VMs with room for snapshots and safety. That said, on a 250GB LUN you may get 9 VMs.

In this scenario, it is really about how much storage you need, how many LUNs you want to manage, the expected I/O on the LUNs and, of course, how many VMs you need in total. If you only need 8 or 9 VMs, create a 250GB LUN and be done with it. If you need 200 VMs, then it would be much simpler to create and manage a smaller number of LUNs at 500GB each than twice that number at 250GB each.

As a general rule, VMFS volumes stored on SANs are between 200 and 500GB. Some environments will go larger or smaller, but from an overall I/O perspective, number of VMs and amount of storage in this range tends to meet the needs of most environments.

Creating VMFS volumes - vCenter

You can create new VMFS volumes from within the vSphere client or from the Service Console of an ESX host.

To create a new VMFS volume using the vSphere client, connect directly to the ESX host or the vCenter server that is managing the ESX host. From the ESX host's Storage link within the Configuration tab, select Add Storage. The following are required steps when creating new VMFS volumes via the wizard:

Select the Storage Type – "Disk/LUN" for block based FC, iSCSI or SCSI devices, "Network File System" for NFS based mount points on your network.

Select Disk/LUN – Select an available disk for creating the VMFS volume.

Current Disk Layout – Select a layout for the disk. VMware recommends using one disk per VMFS volume.

(Note: a single disk in this list is one logical disk, though it may be a set of physical disks logically presented as a single logical entity)

Properties – Enter the datastore name for the new volume

(Note: this name must be unique within the vCenter console)

Formatting – Select a block size for the VMFS volume.

PowerCLI Example

The following shows how PowerCLI can be used to add VMFS datastores to Hosts

```
Cmdlets
New-Datastore

Related Cmdlets
Get-Datastore
Remove-Datastore
Set-Datastore
```

```
EXAMPLE 1:
Add a new "Test Datastore" to the "MyESXHost.mydomain.com".

Get-VMHost "MyESXHost.mydomain.com" | New-Datastore -Vmfs -
Name "Test Datastore" -Path vmhba12:2:1:1
```

Creating VMFS volumes - CLI

You can also create a new VMFS volume from an ESX host console OS by using the vmkfstool command with the -c option.

The following options can be specified when using vmkfstool to create a VMFS volume:

- -b --blocksize – Define the block size for the VMFS-3 file system. The <block_size> value you specify must be 1 MB, 2MB, 4MB, or 8MB.

- -S --setfsname – Define the volume label of a VMFS volume for the VMFS-3 file system you are creating. The label you specify can be up to 128 characters long and cannot contain any leading or trailing blank spaces. This label is also known as the datastore name.

Example:

```
vmkfstools -C vmfs3 -b 2m -S NEWvmfsVolume vmhba1:8:0:2
```

This example illustrates creating a new VMFS-3 datastore named NEWvmfsVolume on the second partition on SCSI target 8, SCSI LUN 0 on apadter vmhba1. The file block size is 2MB.

If your server is managed by vCenter ensure that you have picked a unique name for your VMFS volume even if it is local or only zoned to a single server. vCenter will see this VMFS name and have issues if multiple VMFS volumes show up with the same name.

How should I set up my LUNs on my SAN for ESX?

Configuring SAN storage for your ESX servers is dependent on the type of storage device you plan to use. VMware ESX Server supports a number of different vendors.

To ensure you are deploying your virtual infrastructure with a certified storage area network (SAN), you need to verify your hardware with VMware's compatibility guide. You also need to verify that the SAN devices you are deploying are capable of supporting the vSphere features you are planning to use. Not all storage devices support all vSphere SAN features (e.g., multi-pathing and clustering). Make sure you cross-reference your needs with VMware's SAN feature matrix located in the compatibility guide.

VMware SAN compatibility guide:

http://www.vmware.com/resources/compatibility/pdf/vi_san_guide.pdf

The real trick requires an understanding the general rules associated with different types of storage arrays and the connection protocols. Below is a list of some of the common storage platforms used with ESX and some key items you, as the ESX administrator, should know about:

General LUN/storage key notables

- When presenting LUNs to ESX ensure that each LUN is presented to each and every ESX host in a cluster.

- Ensure that when a LUN is created it is shown to each host with the same LUN ID number.

- Most storage arrays require that you set an OS type. In most cases, Linux or Linux Cluster is the type of OS you will set.

- Active-Passive arrays = Set ESX pathing policy to MRU.

- Active-Active arrays = MRU or fixed pathing policies.

- VMotion is available ONLY IF the source and target hosts are zoned to the same LUNs. VMotion DOES NOT copy disk files between LUNs. It moves the Virtual Machine from one ESX host to another while accessing the same storage location.

- Storage VMotion physically moves storage from one array to another or between available LUNs on a particular array. This means that Storage VMotion also allows for the migration between block based LUNs such and iSCSI and FC to NFS. Storage VMotion can also convert VMs from thick to thinly provisioned models on the fly.

- In the Advanced Settings Panel for ESX hosts in multi-pathed environments, set Disk.UseLunReset to 1 and Disk.UseDeviceReset to 0.

  (Note: for Hosts that contain MSCS Clusters Disk.UseDeviceReset needs to be set to 1!)

- Bigger LUNs mean more VMs per LUN and fewer LUNs to manage. Smaller LUNs mean fewer VMs per LUN and less I/O but more LUNs to manage.

- Major lines supported include; EMC Celerra (a.k.a. Unified Storage), CLARiiON and Symmetrix, HP EVA, XP and MSA, IBM FAStT and Shark, Hitachi Arrays and NetApp

FibreChannel arrays (see SAN compatibility guide for exact versions and models supported).

EMC Symmetrix storage key notables

- Active/Active storage processors (controllers) will allow you to use MRU or Fixed path multi-pathing to balance loads across HBAs and FAs.

- Generally is limited (by EMC recommendation) to physical extents (LUNs) sizes of about 136 GB or so. Could mean a large number of smaller LUNs.

- Disable the SC3 setting. Enable the SPC2 setting for mutli-pathed systems

- VMware requirements for EMC arrays (from their SAN configuration guide):

  ```
  o    Common serial number (C)
  o    Auto negotiation (EAN) enabled
  o    Fibrepath enabled on this port (VCM)
  o    SCSI 3 (SC3)
  o    Unique world wide name (UWN)
  o    SPC-2 (Decal) (SPC2) SPC-2 flag set
  ```

EMC CLARiiON (CX) storage key notables

- Active/Passive storage array so only the MRU policy should be used.

- Does not have the same size limitations on LUNs that a Symmetrix does.

- AX series arrays have more limitations (e.g., RDM and HBA configurations) than the CX series. Consult the current SAN configuration guide for details.

- All Initiator records must have:

  - Failover Mode = 1
  - Initiator Type = "Clariion Open"
  - Array CommPath = "Enabled" or 1

HP MSA storage key notables

- Active/Passive storage array so only the MRU policy should be used.

- Some organizations have reported performance issues with MSAs (1000-series noted) above 2 or 3 ESX hosts.

- Hub controllers have issues using the 2/8 switch or a single controller.

HP EVA storage key notables

- EVA GL is an Active/Passive storage array, so only a policy of MRU should be used.

- EVA XL is Active/Active. You can use MRU or Fixed.

- Connection type on the EVA for ESX hosts should be configured as 000000002200282E for the EVA 3000 and 5000.

- Connection type on the EVA 4000, 6000, or 8000 should be: 000000202200083E.

HP XP storage key notables

- Based on Hitachi platform. See Hitachi documentation.

Hitachi storage key notables

- VERY touchy about configurations, read ALL documentation possible and get updated docs from local rep. Don't read a pocket admin guide for this system.

IBM FAStT (DS 4000)

- Host type should be set to 'LNXCL' Linux Cluster this should disable AVT (Auto Volume Transfer).

For more detailed information, we **HIGHLY** recommend you check out the SAN configuration guide from VMware and your vendor's hardware documentation. ESX and its supporting hardware are constantly changing. As the ESX administrator, you need to ensure the compatibility and supportability of you environment by validating your vendor's currently supported configurations.

Identifying HBA WWNs

In you are planning to connect your ESX environment to a SAN infrastructure one of the things that you will need to do is provide to your SAN administrator is the World Wide Name (WWN) or SAN identifier for the HBA installed in the ESX host. The SAN identifier is used to provision or zone SAN LUNs to your ESX hosts. There are several different ways to get the WWN number that is assigned to your HBA.

The first way to get the WWN assigned to your HBA is by using the vSphere Client connected to either the ESX host directly or via vCenter. Use the following steps to get your WWN or SAN identifier via the vSphere Client:

- Log into the vSphere Client and select the ESX host you wish to get the WWN for.

- Select the Configuration tab and then select the Storage Adapters link.

Listed in the Storage Adapters section will be the HBAs installed in the ESX host and the associated WWN. If your ESX has multiple HBAs installed you see the WWN that is assigned to each adapter port.

PowerCLI Example

The following shows how PowerCLI can be used to identify the WWNs

```
Cmdlets
Get-VMHost
Get-View

Related Cmdlets
Remove-VMHost
Move-VMHost
Set-VMHost
Add-VMHost
Get-VIObjectByVIView

EXAMPLE 1:
Get a list of all WWNs for all HBAs in MyESXHost.mydomain.com

$ESXHost = get-vmhost "MyESXHost.mydomain.com" | Get-View
$storageSystem = get-view $ESXHost.ConfigManager.StorageSystem
$storageSystem.StorageDeviceInfo.HostBusAdapter | select
Device, Model, PortWorldWideName, NodeWorldWideName
```

Configuring ESX to use a NAS/NFS Volume

NFS storage is perfect for VMware environments and has historically been used to host files, ISO images of CDs and DVDs and floppy diskette images amongst other things. Although block based storage devices make up a majority of production VMware implementations NFS and it use as a primary backing for datastores has gained popularity during the last couple of years. Using NFS to hold virtual machines and templates works and is fully supported by VMware. As always, consider the overall workload, performance and availability characteristics when choosing a connectivilty interface.

If you are looking to do some testing in a lab environment and have a UNIX or Linux NFS server available, it is possible to get some shared storage presented to your ESX 4 servers relatively quickly.

Here are some quick notes when using NFS:

1. You must use NFSv3 (SMB/CIFS is not supported)

2. Root access to the NFS mount must not be denied - (no root squash)

3. The NFS mount must be exported with read/write access

To attach your ESX server to an NFS volume, follow these steps:

1. Start the vSphere Client (connect to either a host or the vCenter server)

2. Navigate to the host that you want to setup NFS/NAS storage on

3. Select the Configuration tab

4. Click the Security Profile Link in the Software Panel

5. Click on Properties

6. Check the box next to "NFS Client" and click OK

7. Click on the Storage (SCSI, SAN, NFS) link

8. Click Add Storage in the upper right corner of the work area

9. Choose Network File System and click the Next Button

10. Fill out the information for the NFS server

    Example:

    Server: 10.10.10.15
    Folder: /mnt/esxservers/data/ISO

11. If you do not need write access to the NFS share, click the read only check box (useful if it is only holding NFS shares)

12. Name the Datastore something meaningful, like datastore04_isoLibrary_nfs, and click "Next"

13. Review your data and click Finish when ready

If you receive any errors, ensure the path has been entered correctly into the NFS export and root is not being squashed.

How do I create an iSCSI VMFS Datastore?

Due to the high costs, many organizations elected to implement a NAS device instead of a full blown fabric-based storage area network. Many of the devices support iSCSI. With ESX 4, unchanged from ESX 3, iSCSI volumes can be presented as LUNs. This allows the organization to get into the full capabilities of the vSphere 4 environment without the extra costs of a fabric-based SAN.

Phase 1: Setup Networking

1. Navigate to the server in the inventory pane that will have an iSCSI volume added to it

2. Click on the Configuration Tab

3. Click on the Networking link

4. If you will be using a dedicated NIC(s) for iSCSI traffic, follow these steps:

    a. Click on the Add Networking link

    b. Choose the VMkernel as the Connection Type and click Next

    c. Select the NIC(s) that will be assigned to this vSwitch and click Next

    d. Under Port Group Properties, give the Network Label something meaningful, such as iSCSI Network. Remember to add the VLAN information if you are using VLANs in your environment

    e. If you will be using VMotion for this VMkernel, check Enabled

    f. Add the IP address and subnet information for the VMkernel port

    g. Click on Next

    h. If prompted to enter the default gateway information for the VMkernel Port, enter the correct gateway

Phase 2: Enabling the iSCSI Software Adapter

1. With the vSphere Client still open and on the Configuration tab, click on the Storage Adapters link

2. Click on the iSCSI Software Adapter

3. In the Details section, click on the Properties link

4. The iSCSI Initiator properties window opens

5. Click on the Configure button in the General Tab

6. Check Enabled and click OK

7. When the job is completed, click Close

8. Click on the iSCSI Software adapter

9. Click on Properties in the detail section

10. Click on the Dynamic Discovery tab

11. Click the Add button

12. Enter the TCP/IP address information for the device presenting the iSCSI volumes

13. Change the port only if you have altered it on the Target Device. The default iSCSI target port is: 3260

14. Click OK

15. When the task completes, click on the Close button

16. When prompted to Rescan, do so

17. Click OK; do not change the defaults on the presented panel

18. Once the rescan task is completed, click on the iSCSI software adapter. In the detail section, new LUNs should appear. If there are not any LUNs listed in the detail section, review the TCP/IP address of the iSCSI target to ensure if it is correct. If you are using authentication, click on the Properties link and then the CHAP Authentication tab. Click on Configure to enter the CHAP information as required.

    Click on OK and then Close.

    Once the new task is completed, click on Rescan to see if you can view the new LUNs.

Phase 3: Adding Storage

1. With the vSphere client still open and on the Configuration tab, click on the Storage link in the Hardware portion of the panel

2. Click on the Add Storage link in the upper right hand corner

3. The Add storage wizard will be displayed

4. Select Disk/LUN and click on the Next button

5. Choose the LUN you just added to the Software iSCSI HBA, click Next

6. Review the Disk layout and click on the next button

7. Name the new Datastore, click Next

8. Choose the maximum file size, click Next

9. Review the settings and click Finish

10. Once the task is completed, your new datastore will be ready

Phase 4: Add the iSCSI volume to the remaining servers.

1. Follow Phase one and two

2. Click on the Storage link to see if the storage is available

3. If it is not, Click on Storage Adapters and then the iSCSI Software HBA

4. Click Rescan, the volumes should be available

When the processing has been completed, click on the Summary tab to view your results.

TCP Offload Engine (TOE) Cards

 As of the writing of this guide, TOE Cards, that support hardware based iSCSI Initiator devices, are supported and required if you choose to boot your ESX server from a SAN. Note that TOE and Hardware iSCSI HBAs provide two types of functionality. Together these devices work in-concert to reduce the associated overhead of the TCP/IP stack relative to the physical CPU(s) in an ESX server host. It is important to note however that VMware supports the Hardware iSCSI initiator independently from the ToE functionality. It is the Hardware based iSCSI functionality that ESX leverages for Boot from SAN as this is not possible using a software iSCSI initiator.

The costs associated with TOE cards need to be weighed against the use of standard NICs as ESX provides a great ability to push I/O over standard gigabit Ethernet NICs.

How do I setup iSCSI when the iSCSI network is isolated?

Many organizations do not have a network route between their iSCSI network and their corporate/production LAN. ESX 3 required the Service Console be able to "see" the iSCSI network. This requirement was relaxed with ESXi 3.5 as there is not a Service Console. The iSCSI Service Console is optional with vSphere regardless of the ESX implementation.

For ESX (non-ESXi) implementations, create a Service Console port on the virtual switch configured for iSCSI traffic. This will allow the Service Console to scan for LUN assignments. Complete the same configuration on each ESX 3.5 server that will use iSCSI LUNs on the isolated network.

To add the Service Console Port on the isolated (iSCSI) network, follow these steps:

1. Select an ESX host in the Inventory pane

2. Select the Configuration tab in the work area pane

3. In the Hardware frame, click on the Networking link

4. Click on Properties for the virtual switch that manages the iSCSI traffic

5. The virtual switch properties window opens

6. Click on the "Add…" button

7. Choose Service Console for the Connection type and click next to continue

8. If your iSCSI network has a VLAN ID enter it here otherwise ignore it

9. Enter the IP address information for the second Service Console.

DO NOT CHANGE THE DEFAULT GATEWAY.

Click Next to continue.

10. Review your changes and click finish to complete your changes

Your Service Console should now be able to see your iSCSI LUNs on the isolated network. Remember to rescan for LUN changes under the Storage Adapters link.

Adjusting the HBA Queue depth

 You should only change the Queue Depth if you are experiencing performance problems. When changed, the average queue depth is between 32 and 64 depending on the HBA you are using and some other factors. If you do change the queue depth and do so improperly, severe issues can potentially arise. Always contact support or review current VMware recommendations before changing HBA settings.

A general formula to determine your queue depth setting is shown below:

[Total number of LUNs] * QDepth < [Array queue depth]

To change your queue depth using an esxcfg command you should use the esxcfg-module command as shown below:

```
esxcfg-module -s [setting]=[value] [driver/device]
```

For a qlogic driver we have the example shown below:

```
esxcfg-module -s ql2xmaxqdepth=64 qla2300_7xx
```

Note that after running this command you should run 'esxcfg-boot –b' to ensure that the settings are reloaded after boot. Then Reboot your server

Another option is to edit the esx.conf filed directly. VMware support says they don't recommend this, but if you read the esxcfg command document they also tell you not to run the esxcfg-module command either. The choice is yours. The example below uses a QLogic driver:

1. Back up the file /etc/vmware/esx.conf

2. Edit the /etc/vmware/esx.conf .

3. Locate the options line right under the name line and modify it to specify the maximum queue depth, as follows (where nn

is the queue depth maximum):/device/001:02.0/options = "ql2xmaxqdepth=nn"

4. Repeat for each device/HBA being changed

5. Save your changes and reboot the server.

This process edits the configuration file directly while the first command edits the settings for you without you opening the file. We find it easier just to edit the file and be done with it.

In addition to setting the queue depth, it is highly recommended to adjust the setting "Maximum Outstanding Disk Requests" to the same value. To do this:

1. Open the VI Client and select the host from the inventory panel.

2. Click on the configuration tab, and then under Software click on Advanced Settings.

3. Click on Disk on the left hand side

4. On the right hand side, scroll down and find Disk.SchedNumReqOutstanding.

5. Change the value to match the queue depth.

Replacing/Installing a HBA

Replacing a HBA in ESX 4.0 can be done through the GUI of the vSphere client while connected directly to an ESX host or the vCenter server managing the ESX host.

You should first VMotion any running VMs from the ESX host in which you plan to install/replace an HBA. These steps assume you have two HBAs installed and connectivity to the VMFS still works once you remove one of the two devices.

First enter Maintainence Mode. Power down your ESX host and physically install/replace your HBA. Once you power on your ESX host your configuration steps will be continued from within vCenter.

1. Choose the ESX host to which you added/replaced the HBA

2. Choose the Configuration tab

3. Choose Storage adapters

4. Select Properties link from the Storage Adapters tab

5. Choose Add; the Add adapters wizard starts

6. Select the storage adapter you just installed

7. Choose Next

8. Choose finish at the summary page

You will also need to give the World Wide Name (WWN) of the new HBA to your SAN administrator to associate the HBA to your VMware storage group.

You obtain this from the properties page of the storage adapter.

Alternatively, you can also display the WWN from the Service Console by typing vSphere command; `esxcfg-mpath -a`

Multi-pathing with vSphere and ESX

With vSphere, VMware has introduced multi-pathing functionality for the FibreChannel and iSCSI HBAs that connect an ESX host and its associated network storage. In the basic form, multi-pathing provides for one or more physical paths between host and storage devices to facilitate the transfer of data. The benefits of this configuration option include automatic failover between HBAs and their associated paths, greater scalability, improved availability and increased performance.

VMware has delivered this functionality via the implementation of a greatly enhanced storage I/O subsystem, compared to previous versions of ESX, known as a Pluggable Storage Architecture (PSA). The PSA is an open framework that allows for the use of multiple multi-pathing plugins or MPPs. vSphere ships with an extensible MPP referred to as VMware NMP, Native Multi-Pathing Plugin. NMP manages subplugins available from VMware and third party providers such as EMC and others. At the time of this writing EMC is the only third party multi-pathing provider with a vSphere integrated offering. This offering is known as PowerPath Virtual Edition or PP/VE for short.

Looking at the PSA in greater detail you'll notice there are two types of NMP subplugins; Storage Array Type Plugins (SATPs) and Path Selection Plugins (PSPs). It is within this construct that VMware has enabled third parties to leverage their own multi-pathing offerings for ESX.

According to the VMware, ESX Configuration Guide for vSphere, the PSA performs the following tasks when coordinating NMP with third party MPPs;

- Loads and unloads multi-pathing plugins
- Hides virtual machine specifics from a particular plugin
- Routes I/O requests for a specific logical device to the MPP managing that device
- Handles I/O queuing to the logical devices
- Implements logical device bandwidth sharing between virtual machines
- Handles I/O queuing to the physical storage HBAs.
- Handles physical path discovery and removal
- Provides logical device and physical path I/O statistics.

In addition to the tasks of the PSA, the MPPs are responsible for these operations;

- Manage physical path claiming and unclaiming.
- Manage creation, registration, and deregistration of logical devices.
- Associate physical paths with logical devices.
- Process I/O requests to logical devices.
- Select an optimal physical path for the request .
- Depending on a storage device, perform specific actions necessary to handle path failures and I/O command retries.
- Support management tasks, such as abort or reset of logical devices.

The VMware SATP implements the following tasks;

- Monitors health of each physical path.
- Reports changes in the state of each physical path.
- Performs array-specific actions necessary for storage fail-over.

The VMware PSP is responsible for the actual path selection for a given I/O request.

The VMware NMP assigns a default PSP for every logical device based on the SATP associated with the physical paths for that device. The default PSP can be overridden if there is a need to do so.

By default, the VMware NMP supports the following PSPs:

- **Most Recently Used (MRU)**

  Selects the path the ESX host used most recently to access the given device. If this path becomes unavailable, the host switches to an alternative path and continues to use the new path while it is available.

- **Fixed**

  Uses the designated preferred path, if it has been configured. Otherwise, it uses the first working path discovered at system boot time. If the host cannot use the preferred path, it selects a random alternative available path. The host automatically reverts back to the preferred path as soon as that path becomes available.

  With active-passive arrays that have a Fixed path policy, path thrashing might be a problem.

- **Round Robin (RR)**

  Uses a path selection algorithm that rotates through all available paths enabling load balancing across the paths regardless of existing I/O on a given link.

Of course there are additional options and pathing algorithms available. These will vary based on the third-party provider. The predictive load-balancing algorithm from EMC is a good example of a third-party approach.

Multi-pathing with Local Storage and FibreChannel SAN

In a simple multi-pathing local storage topology, you can use one ESX host, which has two HBAs. The ESX host connects to a dual-port local storage system through two cables. This configuration ensures fault tolerance if one of the connection elements between the ESX host and the local storage system fails (e.g., HBA, cable, port).

To support path switching with FC SAN, the ESX host typically has two or more HBAs available from which the storage array can be reached using one or more switches. Alternatively, the setup can include one HBA and two storage processors so that the HBA can use a different path to reach the disk array.

Multi-pathing with iSCSI SAN

With iSCSI storage, you can take advantage of the multi-pathing support that the TCP/IP network offers. In addition, ESX supports host-based multi-pathing for both hardware and software iSCSI initiators. ESX can use multi-pathing support built into the TCP/IP network, which allows the network to perform routing. Through dynamic discovery, iSCSI initiators obtain a list of target addresses that the initiators can use as multiple paths to iSCSI LUNs for failover purposes. ESX also supports host-based multi-pathing.

With hardware-based iSCSI, the host can have two or more iSCSI HBA and use them as different paths to reach the storage system.

Setting a Path Selection Policy

For each storage device, the ESX host sets the path selection policy based on the claim rules defined in the /etc/vmware/esx.conf file. By default, VMware supports the following path selection policies. If you have a third-party PSP installed on your host, its policy also appears on the list.

Fixed (VMware) - The host always uses the preferred path to the disk when that path is available. If the host cannot access the disk through the preferred path, it tries the alternative paths. The default policy for active-active storage devices is Fixed.

Most Recently Used (VMware) - The host uses a path to the disk until the path becomes unavailable. When the path becomes unavailable, the host selects one of the alternative paths. The host does not revert back to the original path when that path becomes available again. There is no preferred path setting with the MRU policy. MRU is the default policy for active-passive storage devices and is required for those devices.

Changing the Path Selection Policy

Generally, you do not have to change the default multi-pathing settings your host uses for a specific storage device. However, if you want to make any changes, you can use the Manage Paths dialog box to modify a path selection policy and specify the preferred path for the Fixed policy.

Procedure

1. Open the Manage Paths dialog box either from the Datastores or Devices view select a path selection policy

   By default, VMware supports the following path selection policies. If you have a third-party PSP installed on your host, its policy also appears on the list.

   - o Fixed (VMware)
   - o Most Recently Used (VMware)
   - o Round Robin (VMware)

2. For the fixed policy, specify the preferred path by right-clicking the path you want to assign as the preferred path, and selecting Preferred
3. Click OK to save your settings and exit the dialog box

PowerCLI Example

The following shows how PowerCLI can be used to report on policy settings:

```
Cmdlets
Get-VMHost
Get-View

Related Cmdlets
Remove-VMHost
Move-VMHost
Set-VMHost
Add-VMHost
Get-VIObjectByVIView

EXAMPLE 1:
Gets a list of all paths and their policy settings

$ESX = get-vmhost "MyESXHost.mydomain.com" | Get-View

$Information = @()
foreach($disk in $esx.Config.StorageDevice.ScsiLun){
        $MyDetails = "" | Select-Object Name, Policy
        foreach($lun in
$esx.Config.StorageDevice.MultipathInfo.Lun){
        if($disk.CanonicalName -eq $lun.Id){
                        $MyDetails.Name =
$disk.CanonicalName
                        $Mydetails.Policy =
$lun.Policy.Policy
                        $Information += $MyDetails
                }
        }
}
$Information
```

Disable Paths

You can temporarily disable paths for maintenance or other reasons.
You can do so using the vSphere Client.

Procedure

1. Open the Manage Paths dialog box either from the
   Datastores or Devices view
2. In the Paths panel, right-click the path to disable, and select
   Disable
3. Click OK to save your settings and exit the dialog box

You can also disable a path from the adapter's Paths view by right-
clicking the path in the list and selecting Disable.

EMC PowerPath Virtual Edition (PP/VE)

In concert with the vSphere release, EMC released PowerPath/VE
(PP/VE). As of writing of this document it was the only supported and
available multi-pathing plugin, which is the reason why it is the only
multi-pathing plugin described in the document. PP/VE delivers
vSphere integrated; PowerPath multi-pathing features capable of
optimizing ESX pathing to FibreChannel and iSCSI based network
storage. PP/VE allows for the standardization of path management
across heterogeneous physical and VMware environments. Additionally,
PP/VE enables you to automate optimal server, storage, and path
utilization in a dynamic virtual environment. This eliminates the need to
manually load-balance your ESX servers as previously required.

PP/VE differs from and is complementary to NMP from several
different perspectives.

- First of all, PP/VE supports many third party arrays but not
  every one of them. In cases where an unsupported array is
  used with vSphere the standard NMP implementation must
  be used.

  Note: As this document was in development no other
  storage vendor had delivered a vSphere capable multi-
  pathing option. Therefore, the only choices, for the time
  being, are VMware NMP and EMC PP/VE.

- PP/VE supports the following as compared to NMP;

- o Predictive Load Balancing vs. Round Robin
- o Up to 32 Paths vs. 2
- o Up to 8 HBAs vs. 2
- o 3x performance improvement
- o 4x better scalability

There are a number of additional PP/VE features. Please review them here;

- **Auto-restore of paths** — Periodic auto-restore reassigns logical devices when restoring paths from a failed state. Once restored, the paths automatically rebalance the I/O across all active channels.

- **Device prioritization** — Setting a high priority for a single or several devices improves their I/O performance at the expense of the remaining devices, while otherwise maintaining the best possible load balancing across all paths. This is especially useful when there are multiple VMs on a host with varying application performance and availability requirements.

- **Automated performance optimization** — PowerPath/VE automatically identifies the type of storage array and sets the highest performing optimization mode by default.

    - o For Symmetrix, the mode is SymmOpt (Symmetrix Optimized).
    - o For CLARiiON, the mode is CLAROpt (CLARiiON Optimized).
    - o For supported active/active third-party arrays, the mode is Adaptive.

- **Dynamic path failover and path recovery** — If a path fails, PowerPath/VE redistributes I/O traffic from that path to functioning paths. PowerPath/VE stops sending I/O to the failed path and checks for an active alternate path. If an active path is available, PowerPath/VE redirects I/O along that path.

    PP/VE can compensate for multiple faults in the I/O channel (for example, HBAs, fiber-optic cables, a FibreChannel switch, a storage array port).

- **EMC Celerra®, CLARiiON, Symmetrix, and non-EMC array support** — PP/VE supports a wide variety of EMC and non-EMC arrays. Consult the EMC Support Matrix or

E-Lab Navigator for a complete list.

- **Monitor/report I/O statistics** — While PP/VE load balances I/O, it maintains statistics for all I/O for all paths. The administrator can view these statistics using rpowermt.

- **Automatic path testing** — PP/VE periodically tests both live and dead paths.

  - Testing live paths that may be idle, a failed path may be identified before an application attempts to pass I/O down it. By marking the path as failed before the application becomes aware of it, timeout and retry delays are reduced.

  - Testing paths identified as failed, PowerPath/VE will automatically restore them to service when they pass the test. The I/O load will be automatically balanced across all active available paths.

EMC PowerPath Installation and Configuration

The first step in the process requires access to PowerLink, the EMC information portal. The web address is http://powerlink.emc.com. Select PowerPath for VMware from the Software and Downloads Menu as depicted below.

You notice that all of the required components are available in the presented panel. These include the actual PP/VE bits and the management tools for Windows and Linux hosts.

Note: All of the PowerPath documentation is available from Powerlink under the Products tab. Select this tab → PowerPath. Under the Interoperability/Documentation section, click Documentation Library: PowerPath. On the presented panel select PowerPath/VE. Review the Installation and Administration Guide as it contains all of the step-by-step instructions required to facilitate the install

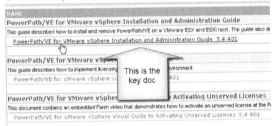

Once you have downloaded the code you need to install the PP/VE loadable module into the VMware vSphere Pluggable Storage Architecture.

Note: EMC is working with VMware to leverage VMware Update Manager (VUM) for installation moving forward. PP/VE is currently VUM enabled for patches and updates.

Procedure:

1. Using the vSphere Virtual Management Assistant (VMA), Login as root to the specific ESX host on which you wish to

install PP/VE

2. Copy the PowerPath/VE file on to the ESX host. Push the file to a temporary location such as /tmp

3. Execute the following command:

   vihostupdate --sever <insert esx host name here> --install --bundle=<Power Path Zip File Name>

   Here is an example using an actual ESX server name and PowerPath file name.

   Note that in this diagram the text wraps at the end of the line.

```
[vi-admin@vma1 tmp]$ vihostupdate --server r805-1.esxdomain.local --install --bu
ndle=EMCPower.VMWARE.5.4.b257.zip_
```

4. When prompted, enter the root credentials
5. The module will take a few moments to install on the host
6. The installation process will present a message that indicates a need to reboot the host. Place the host into Maintenance Mode and reboot. Doing it this way is non-disruptive to the cluster
7. Repeat the process on the other hosts in the ESX cluster
8. Once rebooted, select the ESX server from within vCenter Click Configuration, Select Storage Adapters. Under Details, View: Highlight an available path, move the slider to the right and notice the Owner is listed as PowerPath

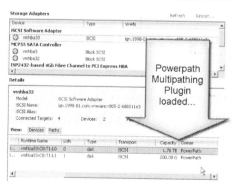

EMC PowerPath - Management Toolset Installation

One of the files you downloaded earlier should have been the management tool for your specific operating system, Windows or Linux. In this text we will focus on the Windows install and configuration.

This installation itself is a straight forward Windows-type install. (e.g., double-click the install icon, next, next, finish)

Once installed, you have a number or PowerPath specific command line tools available.

Next Steps:

1. Check to ensure PowerPath was installed correctly on the ESX host. Issue the following command:

   rpowermt host=<ESX HOST NAME> check_registration

This will check the registration status on the ESX host and provide additional details regarding the PP/VE module.

Note that PowerPath is not licensed. We'll take care of that in a moment.

2. Copy the Host ID string to the clipboard. You will need to this to obtain a license. Use the information in the graphic below…

"Where/How Do I Get A License?"

1) If you are EMC, VMware, or an EMC/VMware partner - email licensekeys@emc.com and ask for PowerPath/VE licenses. You will get a doc, paste in the ESX host IDs. This has a 24hr turnaround.

2) If you are a customer, just ask EMC or an EMC Partner to get you a 45 day trial (Direct Xpress part 456-101-230)

Once you have your license(s) you will need to copy the .lic files into a specific directory on your management host. Using our host from the earlier example; copy the .lic files to the location specified in the installation documentation. In this case we dropped the files into;

C:\Documents and Settings\Administrator\My Documents\EMC\PowerPath\rpowermt

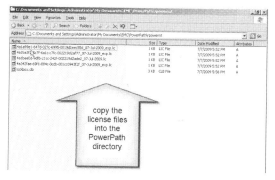

copy the license files into the PowerPath directory

3. Once this is completed you need to register the host. Doing so will enable full PowerPath functionality

The command is:

rpowermt host=<ESX Host Name> register

and this is the expected response:

PowerPath license is registered.

4. Perform these steps for all of the ESX hosts in the cluster on which you installed PowerPath

5. Double check the licensing state using the rpowermt command

```
rpowermt host=<ESX HOST NAME> check_registration
```

6. The screen shot below is an example of the output from this command once all of these steps have been completed.

Notice the State has changed to "licensed" and that, in this case, these licenses are non-expiring.

Thin Provisioning

When you create a virtual machine, a certain amount of storage space on a datastore is provisioned or allocated to the virtual disk files. By default, ESX offers a traditional storage provisioning method during creation in which you estimate how much storage the virtual machine will need for its entire lifecycle, provision a fixed amount of storage space to its virtual disk, and have the entire provisioned space committed to the virtual disk. A virtual disk that immediately occupies the entire provisioned space is called a thick disk. Creating virtual disks in thick format can lead to underutilization of datastore capacity, because large amounts of storage space, pre-allocated to individual virtual machines, might remain unused.

To help avoid over-allocating storage space and save storage, ESX supports thin provisioning,. Using the ESX thin provisioning feature, you can create virtual disks in a thin format. For a thin virtual disk, ESX provisions the entire space required for the disk's current and future activities, but commits only as much storage space as the disk needs for its initial operations.

Virtual Disk Formats

When you perform certain virtual machine management operations, such as create a virtual disk, clone a virtual machine to a template, or migrate a virtual machine, you can specify a format for the virtual disk file.

The following two disk formats are supported;

> Note: You cannot specify the disk format if the disk resides on an NFS datastore. The NFS server determines the allocation policy for the disk.

Thin Provisioned Format: Use this format to save storage space. For the thin disk, you provision as much datastore space as the disk would require based on the value you enter for the disk size. However, the thin disk starts small and at first, uses only as much datastore space as the disk actually needs for its initial operations.

> Note:

> If a virtual disk supports high-level features such as Fault Tolerance, you cannot make the disk thin

> If the thin disk needs more space later, it can grow to its maximum capacity and occupy the entire datastore space provisioned to it

> You can manually convert the thin disk into thick

Thick Format: This is the default virtual disk format. The thick virtual disk does not change its size and from the very beginning occupies the entire datastore space provisioned to it. Thick format does not zero out the blocks in the allocated space.

Create Thin Provisioned Virtual Disks

This procedure assumes that you are creating a typical or custom virtual machine using the New Virtual Machine wizard.

Prerequisites:

You can create thin disks only on the datastores that support thin provisioning. If a disk resides on an NFS datastore, you cannot specify the disk format because the NFS server determines the allocation policy for the disk.

Procedure:

1. In the Create a Disk dialog box, select Allocate and commit space on demand (Thin Provisioning)

A virtual disk in thin format is created. If you do not select the Thin Provisioning option, your virtual disk will have the default thick format.

What to do next:

If you created a virtual disk in the thin format, you can later inflate it to its full size. Simply right click on the VM and select Inflate.

View Virtual Machine Storage Resources

You can view how datastore storage space is allocated for your virtual machines.

Procedure:

1. Select the virtual machine in the inventory
2. Click the Summary tab
3. Review the space allocation information in the Resources section

   o **Provisioned Storage** – Shows datastore space guaranteed to the virtual machine. The entire space might not be used by the virtual machine if it has disks in thin provisioned format. Other virtual machines can occupy any unused space.

   o **Not-shared Storage** – Shows datastore space occupied by the virtual machine and not shared with any other virtual machines.

   o **Used Storage** – Shows datastore space actually occupied by virtual machine files, including configuration and log files, snapshots, virtual disks, and so on. When the virtual machine is running, the used storage space also includes swap files.

Determine the Disk Format of a Virtual Machine

You can determine whether your virtual disk is in thick or thin format.

Procedure:

1. Select the virtual machine in the inventory
2. Click Edit Settings to display the Virtual Machine Properties dialog box
3. Click the Hardware tab and select the appropriate hard disk in the Hardware list

    The Disk Provisioning section on the right shows the type of your virtual disk, either Thin or Thick.

4. Click OK

What to do next:

If your virtual disk is in the thin format, you can inflate it to its full size.

Convert a Virtual Disk from Thin to Thick

If you created a virtual disk in the thin format, vSphere provides the option to convert it to thick. The thin provisioned disk starts small and at first, uses just as much storage space as it needs for its initial operations. You can determine whether your virtual disk is in the thin format and, if required, convert it to thick. After having been converted, the virtual disk grows to its full capacity and occupies the entire datastore space provisioned to it during the disk's creation. For more information on thin provisioning and disk formats, see ESX Configuration Guide or ESXi Configuration Guide.

To determine the disk format of a Virtual Machine perform the following steps:

Procedure:

1. Select the virtual machine in the inventory
2. Click Edit Settings to display the Virtual Machine Properties dialog box

3. Click the Hardware tab and select the appropriate hard disk in the Hardware list. The Disk Provisioning section on the right shows the type of your virtual disk, either Thin or Thick
4. Click OK

What to do next:

If your virtual disk is in the thin format, you can inflate it to its full size.

Convert a Virtual Disk from Thin to Thick

If you created a virtual disk in the thin format, you can convert it to thick.

Procedure:

1. Select the virtual machine in the inventory
2. Click the Summary tab and, under Resources, double-click the datastore for the virtual machine to open the Datastore Browser dialog box
3. Click the virtual machine folder to find the virtual disk file you want to convert. The file has the .vmdk extension
4. Right-click the virtual disk file and select Inflate

The virtual disk in thick format occupies the entire datastore space originally provisioned to it.

Handling Datastore Over-Subscription

Because the provisioned space for thin disks can be greater than the committed space, a datastore over-subscription can occur, which results in the total provisioned space for the virtual machine disks on the datastore being greater than the actual capacity.

Over-subscription can be possible because usually not all virtual machines with thin disks need the entire provisioned datastore space simultaneously. However, if you want to avoid over-subscribing the datastore, you can set up an alarm that notifies you when the provisioned space reaches a certain threshold.

For information on setting alarms, see the VMware Basic System Administration Guide.

If your virtual machines require more space, the datastore space is allocated on a first come first served basis. When the datastore runs out of space, you can add more physical storage and increase the datastore.

Creating a Raw Device Mapping (RDM)

A Raw Device Mapping (RDM) is typically used to when you want to cluster servers with Microsoft Cluster Service when the physical server barrier is crossed (be it between two ESX Servers, two virtual machines on separate hosts, or a virtual machine working in tandem with a physical server).

However, a RDM is useful in other areas as well:

- When a large amount of storage is needed for a virtual machine (typically organizations will create a policy for using RDMs when greater then 100GB is needed)

- When you want to take advantage of SAN technology for mirroring and taking snapshots of data.

RDMs are created in ESX for those situations when you want or need to present a raw LUN to a virtual machine. Think of a RDM as a proxy file that contains a pointer to the actual data that you are trying to access.

During the RDM creation process, a file is created on one of the datastores that holds the metadata for the physical LUN.

Before you can create a Raw Device Mapping, you must present a raw LUN (**NOT A PARTITION**) to the hosts in your ESX cluster. Use the similar process when presenting LUNs for VMFS datastores.

When you map a LUN to a VMFS volume, vCenter Server creates a file that points to the raw LUN. Encapsulating disk information in a file allows vCenter Server to lock the LUN so that only one virtual machine can write to it.

> Note: This file has a .vmdk extension, but the file contains only disk information describing the mapping to the Raw LUN on the ESX/ESXi system. The actual data is stored on the Raw LUN. You cannot deploy a virtual machine from a template and store its data on a Raw LUN. You can only store its data in a virtual disk file.

Procedure:

1. Select a target LUN
2. Select whether you want to store the LUN mapping file on the same datastore as the virtual machine files,

or whether you want to store them on a separate
datastore
3. Select a datastore
4. Select a compatibility mode
5. (Optional) Configure advanced options by selecting a
virtual device node

Virtual Disk Compatibility Modes - Virtual disk compatibility modes
provide flexibility in how a Raw Device Mapping (RDM) LUN
functions.

- **Virtual Compatibility Mode -**

  Virtual mode for an RDM specifies full virtualization of the
  mapped device. It appears to the guest operating system
  exactly the same as a virtual disk file in a VMFS volume.
  The real hardware characteristics are hidden. Virtual mode
  enables you to use VMFS features such as advanced file
  locking and snapshots. Virtual mode is also more portable
  across storage hardware than physical mode, presenting the
  same behavior as a virtual disk file. When you clone the
  disk, make a template out of it, or migrate it (if the migration
  involves copying the disk), the contents of the LUN are
  copied into a virtual disk (.vmdk) file

- **Physical Compatibility Mode -**

  Physical mode for the RDM specifies minimal SCSI
  virtualization of the mapped device, allowing the greatest
  flexibility for SAN management software. In physical mode,
  the VMkernel passes all SCSI commands to the device, with
  one exception: the REPORT LUNs command is virtualized,
  so that the VMkernel can isolate the LUN for the owning
  virtual machine. Otherwise, all physical characteristics of the
  underlying hardware are exposed. Physical mode is useful to
  run SAN management agents or other SCSI target based
  software in the virtual machine. Physical mode also allows
  virtual-to-physical clustering for cost-effective high
  availability. A LUN configured for physical compatibility
  cannot be cloned, made into a template, or migrated if the
  migration involves copying the disk.

Moving a VM between VMFS volumes without vCenter

If you don't have vCenter, there is no other way to move virtual machines between volumes except from the console.

1. Shut down the virtual machine

2. Log onto the COS using PuTTY or another SSH client

3. su if necessary to elevate privileges

4. Un-register the virtual machine using the vmware-cmd command and its VMX file name and location:

   ```
   vmware-cmd -s unregister
   /vmfs/volumes/SOURCE/MyVM/MyVM.vmx
   ```

5. Move the virtual machine using the mv command and its source and target locations

   ```
   mv /vmfs/volumes/SOURCE/MyVM/MyVM
   /vmfs/volumes/TARGET/MyVM/MyVM
   ```

6. Register the virtual machine

   ```
   vmware-cmd -s register
   /vmfs/volumes/TARGET/MyVM/MyVM.vmx
   ```

 When registering the virtual machine, use the LUN IDs, not the Datastore friendly Name.

Paravirtualized SCSI Adapters

Paravirtual SCSI (PVSCSI) adapters are high-performance storage adapters that are capable of providing greater throughput and lower CPU utilization. Paravirtual SCSI adapters are best suited for high performance storage environments. Paravirtual SCSI adapters are not suited for DAS environments. VMware also recommends that you create a primary adapter (non-PVSCSI, LSI Logic by default) for use with the boot disk and a PVSCSI adapter for the disk that will store user data, such as a database.

Paravirtual SCSI adapters are available for virtual machines running hardware version 7 (current for vSphere ESX 4.0) and greater. They are supported on the following guest operating systems:

- Windows Server 2008
- Windows Server 2003

- Red Hat Linux (RHEL) 5

The following features are not supported with Paravirtual SCSI adapters:

- Boot disks
- Record/Replay
- Fault Tolerance
- MSCS Clustering

Paravirtual SCSI adapters have the following limitations:

- Hot-add and Hot-remove requires a bus rescan from within the guest
- Windows guests - In the Computer Management console, right-click Storage → Disk Management and select Rescan Disks
- Linux guests - See the Red Hat Linux Web site for the most current instructions
- Disks on Paravirtual SCSI adapters might not experience performance gains if they have snapshots or if memory on the ESX host is over committed
- If you upgrade from RHEL 5 to an unsupported kernel, you might not be able to access data on the disks attached to a Paravirtual SCSI adapter. To regain access to such disks, run the VMware Tools configuration (vmware-config-tools.pl) with kernel-version parameter and pass the kernel version after the kernel is upgraded and before the virtual machine is rebooted

    Run uname -r to determine the version of the running kernel.

Add a Paravirtualized SCSI Adapter

Prerequisites –

An existing virtual machine with a guest operating system and VMware Tools installed.

Paravirtual SCSI adapters do not support bootable disk. Therefore, the virtual machine must be configured with a primary SCSI adapter to support a disk where the system software is installed.

Procedure:

1. Right-click on the virtual machine and select Edit Setting

2. Click Add
3. Select SCSI Device and click Next
4. Select a SCSI device
5. Select an unused Virtual Device Node
6. Click Next
7. Review your selections and click Finish

A new SCSI device and a new SCSI controller are created

8. Select the new SCSI controller and click Change Type
9. Select VMware Paravirtual and click OK

Migrating VMs with Storage VMotion

Use migration with Storage VMotion to relocate a virtual machine's configuration file and virtual disks while the virtual machine is powered on.

You can change the virtual machine's execution host during a migration with Storage VMotion.

Procedure:

1. Display the virtual machine you want to migrate in the inventory
2. Right-click on the virtual machine, and select Migrate from the pop-up menu
3. Select Change datastore (or Change both host and datastore) and click Next
4. Select a resource pool and click Next
5. Select the destination datastore:

   • To move the virtual machine configuration files and virtual disks to a single destination, select the datastore and click Next

   • To select individual destinations for the configuration file and each virtual disk, click Advanced. In the Datastore column, select a destination for the configuration file and each virtual disk, and click Next.

6. Select a disk format and click Next:

   Option Description:

- **Same as Source** - Use the format of the original virtual disk. If you select this option for an RDM disk in either physical or virtual compatibility mode, only the mapping file is migrated

- **Thin provisioned** - Use the thin format to save storage space. The thin virtual disk uses just as much storage space as it needs for its initial operations. When the virtual disk requires more space, it can grow in size up to its maximum allocated capacity. This option is not available for RDMs in physical compatibility mode. If you select this option for a virtual compatibility mode RDM, the RDM is converted to a virtual disk. RDMs converted to virtual disks cannot be converted back to RDMs.

- **Thick** - Allocate a fixed amount of hard disk space to the virtual disk. The virtualdisk in the thick format does not change its size and from the beginning occupies the entire datastore space provisioned to it. This option is not available for RDMs in physical compatibility mode. If you select this option for a virtual compatibility mode RDM, the RDM is converted to a virtual disk. RDMs converted to virtual disks cannot be converted back to RDMs.

Disks are converted from thin to thick format or thick to thin format only when they are copied from one datastore to another. If you choose to leave a disk in its original location, the disk format is not converted, regardless of the selection made here.

7. Review the page and click Finish.

PowerCLI Example

The following shows how PowerCLI can be used to perform storage VMotion tasks

```
Cmdlets
Get-VM
Move-VM
Get-Datastore

Related Cmdlets
Remove-VM
New-VM
Set-VM
Start-VM
```

```
Stop-VM
Suspend-VM
New-Datastore
Remove-Datastore
Set-Datastore
```

EXAMPLE 1:
Storage VMotion the VM called MyVM to a new datastore called
"MyDatastore"

```
Get-VM "MyVM" |Move-VM -datastore (Get-datastore
"MyDatastore")
```

Monitoring Storage

If you use vCenter Server to manage your ESX/ESXi hosts, you can
review information on storage usage in vCenter Server.

In the vSphere Client, for any inventory object except networking, the
storage usage data appears in the Storage Views tab. To view this tab,
you must have the vCenter Storage Monitoring plug-in, which is
generally installed and enabled by default.

These tools provide you the ability to display storage information in
report form. Reports display relationship tables that provide insight
about how an inventory object is associated with storage entities. They
also offer summarized storage usage data for the object's virtual and
physical storage resources. Use the Reports view to analyze storage
space utilization and availability, multi-pathing status, and other storage
properties of the selected object and items related to it.

> For more information on virtual and physical storage
> resources and how virtual machines access storage, see
> the VMware ESX Configuration Guide or ESXi
> Configuration Guide.

Looking at Storage Reports in greater detail we understand that this
functionality will display statistics for different categories and inventory
objects. For example, if the inventory object is a datastore, you can
display information for all virtual machines that reside on the datastore,
all hosts that have access to the datastore, the LUNs on which the
datastore is deployed, and so on. When you display the report tables,
the default column headings depend on the inventory object you select.
You can customize the tables by adding or removing columns. Reports
are updated every 30 minutes. You can manually update the reports by
clicking Update.

You can search for specific information you need to see by filtering
report tables based on storage attributes and keywords. Reports may

also be filtered, exported and customized. The following steps will review the steps required to display a particular report.

Displaying Storage Reports:

You display storage reports to review storage information for any inventory object except networking. For example, if the inventory object is a virtual machine, you can review all datastores and LUNs that the virtual machine uses, status of all paths to the LUNs, adapters that the host uses to access the LUNs, and so on.

Procedure:

1. Display the object, for which you want to view reports, in the inventory.

   For example, display virtual machines if you want to review storage information for a specific virtual machine.

2. Select the object and click Storage Views → Reports.

3. To display information for a specific category, click Show all [Category of Items] and select the appropriate category from the list.

   For example, if you want to see all datastores that the virtual machine is using, select Show all Datastores.

4. To see the description of each column, move the cursor over the column heading.

Security

The security section (much like the network section) is not really here to define your best practices or say how you should secure your environment. We will also not be focusing on VMsafe or vShield Zones in this chapter. Instead, this section just focuses on the ways to do certain tasks that we feel fall into a security context (such as authentication) and relate to securing your hypervisor.

There are tasks in this section that your security folks may not be happy with (like re-enabling root access over SSH). We are not recommending that you do this to every server. Rather, this section provides information on how to perform the tasks. As always, validate each task in your lab environment first and against your own internal policies.

What's new?

vSphere 4.0 introduces Memory Hardening, Kernel Module Integrity and of course extended permissions for vCenter!

Memory Hardening basically means that drivers, libraries, applications and even the ESX kernel are stored in random memory locations. This location is non-predictable which makes the hypervisor less vulnerable for memory exploits and malicious code.

Authenticity of modules, drivers and applications are assured by a digital signature. This signature will be verified when the modules, driver or application is loaded by the VMkernel.

Datastore privileges enables you to control who does what on which datastore. One of the most used privileges will most likely be "Allocate space". With "Allocate space" one can control who can create new virtual machines, snapshots, clone or create a new virtual disk on a specific datastore.

Privileges can also be controlled for Distributed vSwitched and Distributed Portgroups. With Distributed vSwitches setting the correct permissions has become a lot more important because of the risk and impact changing a vDS or portgroup has.

Creating a local user account

Creating a new user account can be done from the GUI or from the console. To create a user from the GUI, you'll need to connect directly to the server using the vSphere Client. You cannot create a user on a server while connected to the vCenter server.

Navigate to the Users & Groups tab and then right-click on the right side of the screen. Select Add, type in the user name, and set a strong password.

To create a new user from the command line (console session), connect to the server using PuTTY, use sudo to elevate your privileges, and then run the useradd command:

```
useradd -m user1
```

To set a password for the user, add the –p switch

```
useradd -m user1 -p astrongpassword
```

If this is a local user only (not a matching user here for use with something like the Kerberos PAM) make sure you set a password with the –p option

 If you plan on using PAM for authentication, you'll have to set up the user accounts from the console, since the GUI doesn't allow you to add accounts with null or blank passwords.

PowerCLI Example

The following shows how PowerCLI can be used to create the local user account.

Note: You need to connect directly to the ESX host for this script to work.

Cmdlets
```
New-VMHostAccount
```

Related Cmdlets
```
Get-VMHostAccount
Set-VMHostAccount
```

EXAMPLE 1:
```
Adds a new local user on ESX host ESXSRV1:

Connect-VIServer ESXSRV1
New-VMHostAccount -ID User1 -Password pass -UserAccount
```

Enabling SSH access for root

ESX 4.x installs with SSH access disabled for root. This is a common best practice for both Linux as well as Unix-based systems and should be left disabled. However, if you do need to enable it, follow the below procedures:

1. Log into the local console of the ESX hos

2. Edit the file /etc/SSH/SSHd_config (you
    nano, though nano is the easiest for novices

3. Find the line PermitRootLogin and change it

4. Use Ctrl-O to write out the file, then close nano.

5. At the console run /etc/init.d/SSHd restart to restart the
    SSH daemon.

If you are going to leave SSH enabled for root, ensure that the
password:

-   Has both upper and lowercase letters

-   Has digits, punctuation marks, or other symbols

-   Is not based on your login

-   Is not a real word

-   Is at least seven or eight characters long.

 **Consider using a regular user account for SSH access
instead of root. You can always su after you connect
for root access or use sudo to run commands with the
appropriate permissions.**

Resetting the root password

Resetting the root password is a fairly simple operation if you know the
existing root password. Also in this section we outline resetting the
password not recovering for a lost password (covered in another how
to).

To reset the root password using the vSphere Client

1. Log on connecting locally to the ESX host through vSphere
    Client

2. Select the Host from inventory

3. Choose the Users and Groups tab and select users.

4. Right-click on root and select edit.

5. A user box for root appears.

6. Select Change Password and type the password and confirm it.

7. Select ok.

From the Console login as the root user and run the command 'passwd'. You will be prompted for the new root password.

PowerCLI Example

The following shows how PowerCLI can be used to reset the password for the root account.

Note: You need to connect directly to the ESX host for this script to work.

Cmdlets
```
Set-VMHostAccount
```

Related Cmdlets
```
Get-VMHostAccount
New-VMHostAccount
```

EXAMPLE 1:
```
Sets the password for the Root user account on ESX host
ESXSRV1:

Connect-VIServer ESXSRV1
Set-VMHostAccount -UserAccount Root -Password NewPass123
```

Recovering the root password

This procedure is used for recovery of a lost or unknown root password. It should NOT be used to reset the password if you already know it.

If you lost your root password and need to change it you must have physical access to the server (either at its console or via some type of KVM system) and have the ability to shut down the server (so note there may be an interruption of service if you don't VMotion off the VMs).

1. When the ESX host boots to the grub menu, select "a."

2. Enter "single" at the prompt.

3. Select Enter.

4. At the prompt type "passwd."

5. Enter your new password.

6. Type "reboot."

7. Log in with your new root password.

Using AD for ESX user passwords

In order for you to allow user accounts to use Active Directory for authentication when accessing the console, you need to configure what is call PAM authentication. If you have ever set up PAM authentication on an ESX host you know that even though the process is pretty straightforward, something always seems to go wrong. VMware has tried to simplify the process of PAM configuration by presenting us with a command called esxcfg-auth. For the most part, they've succeeded.

In order to get the PAM configuration up and running, you will need to make sure that a couple of other things are configured first. Start by making sure that DNS name resolution is correctly configured (/etc/resolve.conf). Make sure that you can resolve the FQDN of the domain and the domain controllers that you are going to use for your PAM configuration. You will also need to make sure that the time is correctly configured on the ESX host. If the time is off even by as little as five minutes, your Kerberos authentication may fail. This would be a good time to configure and enable NTP if you have not already done so.

Before we get into the command details, you need to understand that this only provides you central management of passwords. You still need to create the user accounts locally on the ESX host. The following is an example of the command used to create a user account from the console of an ESX host:

```
/usr/sbin/useradd joeuser
```

Now that we have a local user account, let's configure the ESX server to use Active Directory to verify joeuser's password. The following command is an example of configuring the ESX host to authenticate users against an Active Directory domain called mydomain.com, using a DC named mydc:

```
/usr/sbin/esxcfg-auth --enablead --adddomain mydomain.com --
addc mydc.mydomain.com --krb5realm=mydomain.com --krb5kdc
mydc.mydomain.com --krb5adminserver mydc.mydomain.com
```

We would advise that you use the —addc switch multiple times to add more than one domain controller to the list. Now let's break down each section of this command and describe its function:

- (--enablead) Enables AD Authentication
- (--adddomain) Domain name of the domain that you wish to use for authentication.
- (--addc) Name of the domain controller for this configuration.
- (--krb5realm=) Name of the Kerberos realm, which is the same as the domain name.

- (--krb5kdc) Name of the domain controller that Kerberos is going to use for key distribution server.
- (krb5adminserver) adds the server that Kerberos will use for administrative services.

This configuration enables system-wide password authentication via Active Directory on the ESX host. If you want to use PAM authentication for users who access the ESX host directly via the vSphere Client, you will need to grant permissions to those users first by using the permissions tab in the client.

Your ESX environment should now be configured to use Active Directory for password authentication. If you have problems with PAM authentication, you can start your troubleshooting process by reviewing the /var/log/messages and /var/log/security logs for error messages.

 If you plan on using PAM authentication for your ESX servers make sure that you do not have an account in Active Directory named root. PAM authentication affects all authentication, even the root account, and would allow someone to change the password to this account in Active Directory and gain root access to all of your ESX hosts.

Password complexity

The default password policy in terms of complexity and for instance password age is limited. We recommend changing at least the following settings to improve security:

Set the maximum number of days the password is valid, we recommend 60 days:

```
esxcfg-auth --passmaxdays=60
```

Set the minimum number of days the password remains valid, we recommend 1 day:

```
esxcfg-auth --passmindays=1
```

Set the number of days a warning is given before a password expires, we recommend 15 days:

```
esxcfg-auth --passwarnage=15
```

Set the password complexity and for instance the amount of retries. The format should be:

```
esxcfg-auth --usecrack=<retries> <minimum_length> <lc_credit>
<uc_credit> <d_credit> <oc_credit>
```

Where LC stands for "lowercase", UC for "uppercase", "d" for "digit" and "oc" for special character.

We recommend a maximum of 3 retries and a minimum password length of 8:

```
esxcfg-auth --usecrack=3 8 0 0 0 0
```

Keep in mind that if you add a level of complexity, for instance at least 2 uppercase characters, this will be subtracted from the password length. So for instance the following command will result in a password of 6 characters if two uppercase characters are used:

```
esxcfg-auth --usecrack=3 8 0 2 0 0
```

Configuring sudo on your ESX server

If you are in an enterprise environment where the root account and password is a closely guarded secret, the use of sudo will allow other ESX administrators the full use of the command line with out the need of the root password.

sudo allows a user to self elevate their privileges having root execute a command on the users behalf. The typical syntax is in this form:

```
sudo /usr/sbin/esxcfg-nics -l
```

However, having to type all that on the command line is rather cumbersome. Thankfully, the alias command can save us from having to type all that. Alias allows us to create a shortcut command:

```
alias esxcfg-nics='sudo /usr/sbin/esxcfg-nics'
```

The format of the alias command is important. If you put spaces around the equals (=) sign, the alias command will fail. Using a non-root account, the command can now successfully be executed as:

```
esxcfg-nics -l
```

Of course, it is possible and common to run the following command as a direct replacement for the su command:

```
sudo su -
```

Setting up sudo is done by executing the visudo command as root. The following /etc/sudoers file is a good sample to start with (refer to http://www.gratisoft.us/sudo/ for more information):

```
#
# Sample /etc/sudoers file for the ESX commands.
#
# This file MUST be edited with the 'visudo' command as root.
```

```
#
# See the sudoers man page for the details on how to write a
sudoers file.
#

User_Alias ESXADMINS = dan, kevin, don
User_Alias ESXSUPPORT = ron, steve
User_Alias ESXOPS = esxoperator

Cmnd_Alias ESXADM = /usr/sbin/, /usr/bin/
Cmnd_Alias ESXCFG = /usr/sbin/esxcfg-advcfg, \
    /usr/sbin/esxcfg-auth, /usr/sbin/esxcfg-boot, \
/usr/sbin/esxcfg-dumppart, /usr/sbin/esxcfg-firewall \
/usr/sbin/esxcfg-info, /usr/sbin/esxcfg-init, \
/usr/sbin/esxcfg-linuxnet, /usr/sbin/esxcfg-module, \
/usr/sbin/esxcfg-mpath, /usr/sbin/esxcfg-nas, \
/usr/sbin/esxcfg-nics, /usr/sbin/esxcfg-rescan, \
/usr/sbin/esxcfg-resgrp, /usr/sbin/esxcfg-route, \
/usr/sbin/esxcfg-swiscsi, /usr/sbin/esxcfg-upgrade, \
/usr/sbin/esxcfg-vmhbadevs, /usr/sbin/esxcfg-vmknic, \
/usr/sbin/esxcfg-vswif, /usr/sbin/esxcfg-vSwitch, \
/usr/sbin/esxupdate
Cmnd_Alias VMKTLS = /usr/sbin/vmkchdev, /usr/sbin/vmkdump, \
    /usr/sbin/vmkfstools, /usr/sbin/vmkiscsid, \
    /usr/sbin/vmkiscsi-device, /usr/sbin/vmkiscsi-iname, \
    /usr/sbin/vmkiscsi-ls, /usr/sbin/vmkiscsi-tool, \
    /usr/sbin/vmkiscsi-util, /usr/sbin/vmkloader, \
    /usr/sbin/vmkload_mod, /usr/sbin/vmklogger, \
    /usr/sbin/vmkpcidivy, /usr/sbin/vmkping
Cmnd_Alias UTILS = /bin/kill, /sbin/shutdown, /sbin/reboot, \
    /usr/bin/esxtop, /usr/bin/top, /sbin/ifconfig

Defaults syslog=auth, log_year, logfile=/var/log/sudo.log
Defaults:ESXADMINS !lecture
Defaults:dan     !authenticate

root                ALL = (ALL) ALL
%wheel              ALL = (ALL) ALL
ESXADMINS  ALL = NOPASSWD: ESXADM,!/usr/bin/passwd root
ESXSUPPORT ALL = NOPASSWD: ESXCFG, VMKTLS, UTILS, \
    !/usr/bin/passwd root
ESXOPS ALL = ESXCFG, VMKTLS, UTILS,!/usr/bin/passwd root
+NOC ALL = /usr/bin/su esxoperator
ALL ALL = NOPASSWD: /bin/umount /mnt/cdrom, \
    /bin/umount /mnt/floppy,     /bin/mount /mnt/cdrom, \
    /bin/mount /mnt/floppy \
```

The above example allows users in the ESXADMINS user alias the
ability to use sudo to execute every command in the /usr/bin and
/usr/sbin directories.

Take note of the change in the defaults section. Each command that is
executed via sudo is logged to /var/log/sudo.log. An audit trail will be
created, allowing you to backtrack should something happen to your
ESX server.

Remember the alias command? Wouldn't it be great to be able to have
each command mapped to an alias at login? Let's take a look at the
.bashrc file. This resource file is sourced for you at login when your
login shell is bash. To get new users the ability to use the alias mappings

at login, the /etc/skel/.bashrc needs to be edited as root. Using the file editor of your choice, update the file to look like this:

```
# .bashrc

# User specific aliases and functions

alias     esxcfg-advcfg='sudo /usr/sbin/esxcfg-advcfg'
alias     esxcfg-auth='sudo /usr/sbin/esxcfg-auth'
alias     esxcfg-boot='sudo /usr/sbin/esxcfg-boot'
alias     esxcfg-dumppart='sudo /usr/sbin/esxcfg-dumppart'
alias     esxcfg-firewall='sudo /usr/sbin/esxcfg-firewall'
alias     esxcfg-info='sudo /usr/sbin/esxcfg-info'
alias     esxcfg-init='sudo /usr/sbin/esxcfg-init'
alias     esxcfg-linuxnet='sudo /usr/sbin/esxcfg-linuxnet'
alias     esxcfg-module='sudo /usr/sbin/esxcfg-module'
alias     esxcfg-mpath='sudo /usr/sbin/esxcfg-mpath'
alias     esxcfg-nas='sudo /usr/sbin/esxcfg-nas'
alias     esxcfg-nics='sudo /usr/sbin/esxcfg-nics'
alias     esxcfg-rescan='sudo /usr/sbin/esxcfg-rescan'
alias     esxcfg-resgrp='sudo /usr/sbin/esxcfg-resgrp'
alias     esxcfg-route='sudo /usr/sbin/esxcfg-route'
alias     esxcfg-swiscsi='sudo /usr/sbin/esxcfg-swiscsi'
alias     esxcfg-upgrade='sudo /usr/sbin/esxcfg-upgrade'
alias     esxcfg-vmhbadevs='sudo /usr/sbin/esxcfg-vmhbadevs'
alias     esxcfg-vmknic='sudo /usr/sbin/esxcfg-vmknic'
alias     esxcfg-vswif='sudo /usr/sbin/esxcfg-vswif'
alias     esxcfg-vSwitch='sudo /usr/sbin/esxcfg-vSwitch'
alias     esxtop='sudo /usr/sbin/esxtop'
alias     esxupdate='sudo /usr/sbin/esxupdate'
alias     kill='sudo /bin/kill'
alias     shutdown='sudo /sbin/shutdown'
alias     reboot='sudo /sbin/reboot'
alias     esxtop='sudo /usr/bin/esxtop'
alias     top='sudo /usr/bin/top'
alias     ifconfig='sudo /sbin/ifconfig'
alias     ethtool='sudo /sbin/ethtool'
alias     vmkchdev='sudo /usr/sbin/vmkchdev'
alias     vmkdump='sudo /usr/sbin/vmkdump'
alias     vmkfstools='sudo /usr/sbin/vmkfstools'
alias     vmkiscsid='sudo /usr/sbin/vmkiscsid'
alias     vmkiscsi-device='sudo /usr/sbin/vmkiscsi-device'
alias     vmkiscsi-iname='sudo /usr/sbin/vmkiscsi-iname'
alias     vmkiscsi-ls='sudo /usr/sbin/vmkiscsi-ls'
alias     vmkiscsi-tool='sudo /usr/sbin/vmkiscsi-tool'
alias     vmkiscsi-util='sudo /usr/sbin/vmkiscsi-util'
alias     vmkloader='sudo /usr/sbin/vmkloader'
alias     vmkload_mod='sudo /usr/sbin/vmkload_mod'
alias     vmklogger='sudo /usr/sbin/vmklogger'
alias     vmkpcidivy='sudo /usr/sbin/vmkpcidivy'
alias     vmkping='sudo /usr/sbin/vmkping'

# Source global definitions
if [ -f /etc/bashrc ]; then
  . /etc/bashrc
fi
```

When new users are created, their default .bashrc file will contain the alias mapping.

Although the alias commands will work for new users, existing users will need to have their current .bashrc file updated.

The alternative way is to edit the global bash resource file, /etc/bashrc. This would give the aliases to each user at every login. Adding some code around group checking, alias mapping could be created only for users that needed them during the login process.

 A word of caution here – remapping files in this manner will mask the underlying command. When the user executes the command, it will be run as root. There is a degree of trust as you allow fellow coworkers the ability to execute commands as root on your ESX server. Make sure you are logging the sudo commands!

Modifying the host firewall

Everything is done for a reason. This is especially true with ESX 3.x (and higher) having its own firewall. Administration versus security is a constant battle, so you should only enable what you absolutely need.

The firewall (based on iptables) on each host can be configured from either the GUI or from the console/command line. To modify the firewall rules from the GUI, use the vSphere Client and navigate to the Configuration tab and then select Security Profile. The GUI will only allow you to configure a handful of known services/ports (suspicious things like LDAP were not even available in beta versions). Anyway, if you have a specific application that isn't allowed, you'll need to go to the console.

To change the firewall rules from the console, first SSH into the host and use the esxcfg-firewall command located in /usr/sbin. The command can enable specific known services as well as specific ports. We also should note here that esxcfg-firewall.log is located in /var/log/vmware.

Some common items that you'll need to enable include:

- **SSH Client –** this allow you use SSH from the ESX host, which is required for SCP and third-party applications like Vizioncore's esxRanger to function.

```
esxcfg-firewall -e SSHClient
```

- **Monitoring software** such as HP Systems Insight Manger and Dell OpenManage will require some of the below ports opened.

SNMP

```
esxcfg-firewall -e snmpd
```

Dell OpenManage

```
esxcfg-firewall -o 1311,tcp,in
```

HP RDP/Altiris

```
esxcfg-firewall -o 402,tcp,in
esxcfg-firewall -o 402,tcp,out
```

- **Authentication** – If you're using AD / LDAP / Kerberos authentication, then you'll need to open some of these ports.

Kerberos

```
esxcfg-firewall -e activedirectorKerberos
esxcfg-firewall -e kerberos
```

LDAP

```
esxcfg-firewall -e LDAP
```

- **NTP** – This port is needed for time synchronization.

```
esxcfg-firewall -e ntpClient
```

You can list all other known services with the following command:
esxcfg-firewall -s

To open all ports on the firewall, which is NOT recommended but could be useful for troubleshooting, you should execute:

```
esxcfg-firewall --allowIncoming
esxcfg-firewall --allowOutgoing
```

PowerCLI Example

The following cmdlets and examples show how PowerCLI can be used to manage the ESX firewall:

Cmdlets
```
Get-VMHostFirewallException
Get-VMHostFirewallDefaultPolicy
Set-VMHostFirewallException
Set-VMHostFirewallDefaultPolicy
```

EXAMPLE 1:
Retrieves the enabled firewall exceptions of the ESX host with a name of ESXSRV1:

```
Connect-VIServer VISRV
```

```
Get-VMHostFirewallException -VMHost (Get-VMHost -Name ESXSRV1)
-Enabled $true | Format-List

New-VMHostAccount -ID User1 -Password pass -UserAccount
```

EXAMPLE 2:
Retrieves the default firewall policy of the ESX host with an
name of ESXSRV1:

```
Connect-VIServer VISRV
Get-VMHostFirewallDefaultPolicy -VMHost (Get-VMHost -Name
ESXSRV1)
```

EXAMPLE 3:
Enables a firewall exception for the NTP Client on ESXSRV1:

```
Connect-VIServer VISRV
Get-VmhostFirewallException -VMHost ESXSRV1 -Name "NTP Client"
| Set-VMHostFirewallException -enabled:$true
```

Logging on to your ESXi console

Although this is unsupported we did want to mention that it's possible
to login to the ESXi console. This is normally used as a backdoor for
support only:

1. Log in to your ESX Server 3i at the console.
2. Press Alt+F1 to switch to the console window.
3. Enter unsupported to start the Tech Support Mode login
   process. Note that no text will appear on the console
   window.
4. Enter the password for the root user. Tech Support Mode is
   now active.
5. Complete tasks in Tech Support Mode.
6. Enter the command exit to exit Tech Support Mode.
7. Press Alt+F2 to return the server to DCUI mode.

ESXi and SSH

Now that you know how to open up the ESXi console it is also possible
to open it up for SSH. Again this is not recommended and it is not
supported but might come in handy when troubleshooting your
environment:

1. Go to the ESXi console and press alt+F1
2. Type: unsupported
3. Enter the root password (No prompt, typing in blindly)

4. At the prompt edit the inetd.conf file
   ```
   vi /etc/inetd.conf
   ```
5. Look for the line that starts with "#SSH" (you can search with pressing "/")
6. Remove the "#" (press the "x" if the cursor is on the character)
7. Save "/etc/inetd.conf" by typing
   ```
   :wq!
   ```
8. Kill the inet.d daemon to reload the config file:
   ```
   ps | grep inetd
   kill -hup <process id>
   ```

PowerCLI

Throughout this guide you will notice PowerCLI examples, these have been added to show how automation can be made easy, and everything that can be done from the GUI can be automated through the use of PowerCLI.

PowerCLI is an add-on or what is known as a PowerShell snap-in.

What is PowerShell ?

PowerShell or Windows PowerShell is an extensible command-line shell and associated scripting language created by Microsoft for Microsoft Windows operating systems.

Windows PowerShell was released in 2006 and is currently available for Windows XP SP2/SP3, Windows Server 2003, Windows Vista, and is included in Windows Server 2008 as an optional feature.

Windows PowerShell 2.0 was released with Windows 7 and Windows Server 2008 R2. It is going to be backported to previous supported platforms Windows XP SP3, Windows Server 2003 SP2, Windows Vista SP1 and Windows Server 2008.

Windows PowerShell integrates with the Microsoft .NET Framework and provides an environment to perform administrative tasks by execution of cmdlets (pronounced commandlets).

All demonstrations in this book have been written in Windows PowerShell V1 but will also work in V2.

To teach you how to use Windows Powershell from beginning to end is out of scope of this guide and is best left to the areas mentioned later in the Getting Help part of this chapter.

Installing PowerCLI

Where should I install PowerCLI ?

PowerCLI can work from any windows machine, which supports Windows PowerShell, PowerCLI does not need to be installed on your vCenter server or even on a workstation with the vCenter client in order for it to work.

Step by Step guide to installing PowerCLI

Before installing Windows Powershell the .Net framework v2.0 at least will need to be downloaded and installed.

This is a Next, Next, Next setup wizard which should be followed through until completed.

Following the installation of the framework Windows PowerShell for XP/Vista/2003 will need to be downloaded, for Windows 2008 this will come pre-installed and can be added as a feature. This can be downloaded and installed from the following site: http://www.microsoft.com/windowsserver2003/technologies/management/powershell/download.mspx

This is also a Next, Next, Next setup wizard which should be followed until completely installed.

Once PowerShell has been installed the execution policy will need to be configured. As Windows PowerShell was written as a secure scripting language an execution policy should be chosen and set using the Set-ExecutionPolicy cmdlet.

The following are valid options for the execution policy:

- AllSigned
  All scripts as well as configuration files must be signed by a trusted publisher. This includes script on the local as well as remote machines.

- Default
  Uses the default restricted policy.

- RemoteSigned
  All scripts as well as configuration files downloaded via the Internet must be signed by a trusted publisher.

- Restricted
  This is the PowerShell default and will not allow you to execute scripts or load configuration files.

- Unrestricted
  This allows you to execute all scripts as well as load configuration files.

As a minimum it is recommended that the execution policy be set to remotesigned, this can be done by issuing the following cmdlet with parameters at the PowerShell prompt:

```
Set-ExecutionPolicy remotesigned
```

Once these have been installed VMware PowerCLI can be downloaded from www.vmware.com/go/powershell, follow through the installation wizard until PowerCLI has been installed.

PowerCLI is currently version 4.0.0 | 05/21/09 | 162509 as of writing this guide.

Once the installation has completed a new icon will appear on your
desktop and on your start menu called 'VMware vSphere PowerCLI'.
Now the magic can begin!

PowerCLI Basics

You have installed PowerCLI and double clicked on the 'VMware
vSphere PowerCLI' icon, you have been presented with a nice black box
and some pretty yellow and green text, what now?

There are some cmdlets designed to help you get started:

- **Get-VICommand**

  This will give you a list of all cmdlets which have been
  written to use with the virtual infrastructure in different
  ways, these are used throughout this book and are listed
  before each example is given.

- **Get-VIToolkitDocumentation**

  This will open a vSphere PowerCLI cmdlets reference GUI
  help file which can be used to find reference for each cmdlet
  including full details and examples of how to use these.

- **Connect-VIServer**

  By far the most important cmdlet in PowerCLI.

  This cmdlet is used to make a connection to a vCenter
  Server or ESX host, if you launched PowerCLI as a user
  who has permissions to the vCenter server your credentials
  will be passed along with the cmdlet to make a connection,
  optional parameters can be passed to the cmdlet to supply

alternate connection credentials or supply a different port from the default as below:

```
Connect-VIServer -Server MyVIServer -Port 8443 -User
"myuser" -Password "mypassword"
```

Once your server session is established, you are able to use the rest of the provided cmdlets. For example, to browse the virtual machines on the server, run the following cmdlet:

```
Get-VM
```

Try some of the other cmdlets and see what happens, a good place to start is with the Get- cmdlets, these are the cmdlets which are for gathering information and returning it to the console.

Object Orientated Language

What does this mean, I am not a developer why am I bothered?

You may not understand what an object orientated language is but it is best to remember that the information you are getting back from these cmdlets and everything in Powershell is object orientated, this means that often the results you see will be just a subset of the real information that is being returned, for example:

When typing get-vm you will receive the following:

```
PS C:\> get-vm

Name                    PowerState Num CPUs Memory (MB)

----                    ---------- -------- -----------

Testvm01                PoweredOn  1        2048

Testvm2                 PoweredOff 1        2048
```

But this is just a subset of the real information, to gain more information about what lies beneath we can push (or as it is known in Powershell, pass the cmdlet down the pipeline) the get-vm cmdlet to a cmdlet native to PowerShell called Get-Member as below:

```
Get-VM | Get-Member
```

This will return the real information including both properties (the information) and methods (things you can do with that returned object).

For more information on Get-Member type: `get-help get-member -detailed`

So now for example we can choose some more information to show:

```
PS C:\> get-vm | Select-Object Name, NumCpu, MemoryMB,
HardDisks, Description

Name        : testvm01

NumCpu      : 1

MemoryMB    : 2048

HardDisks   : {Hard Disk 1}

Description : Domain Controller


Name        : testvm02

NumCpu      : 1

MemoryMB    : 2048

HardDisks   : {Hard Disk 1, Hard Disk 2}

Description : File Server
```

Remember this is just a quick guide, for more information on
PowerShell and its fundamentals make sure you check out the Microsoft
PowerShell site:
http://www.microsoft.com/windowsserver2003/technologies/manage
ment/powershell/default.mspx

A great book reference is 'Windows PowerShell in Action by Bruce
Payette' which can be purchased here:
http://www.amazon.co.uk/Windows-PowerShell-Action-Bruce-
Payette/dp/1932394907

Using the Examples

Throughout this book examples of PowerCLI have been displayed
detailing how to perform certain actions or gather information, to use
these examples simply change the information where relevant, copy and
paste them into the PowerCLI console and sit back whilst the magic
begins. A zip file of all of these scripts is available at:

http://www.yellow-bricks.com/wp-content/uploads/quickstartguide.zip

Various PowerShell Editors can also be used to run and debug these
scripts including the free script editor, which comes with the
Virtualization EcoShell as mentioned later in this chapter.

All reporting scripts within this quick start guide have also been
designed to output as a single object, what this means is that these can
easily be used to output to your chosen format, you can use the Export-
CSV, ConvertTo-CSV, ConvertTo-Html, ConvertTo-XML on the end
of each example as per the below example:

```
Connect-VIServer TESTVC
$VMTools = @()
Foreach ($VM in (Get-VM)){
        $MyDetails = "" | Select-Object Name, Tools
        $MyDetails.Name = $vm.Name
        $MyDetails.Tools = $vm.config.tools.toolsVersion
        $VMTools += $MyDetails
}
$VMTools | Export-CSV "C:\Temp\VMTools.csv"
```

 Dont forget to use the connect-viserver cmdlet to connect to your vCenter server or host before using the examples.

PowerCLI Mastery

This chapter takes you through a miniscule amount of information when it comes to PowerCLI and PowerShell, to release the full potential of PowerCLI it is recommended you read 'Managing VMware Infrastructure With Windows PowerShell' by Hal Rottenberg which can be purchased from here:
http://www.amazon.com/dp/0982131402/ref=cm_sw_su_dp

" In "Managing VMware Infrastructure With Windows PowerShell", you will learn how to perform everything from simple ad-hoc reporting at the command-line ("Are any of my virtual machines powered off?") to complex scripts to automate a massive deployment of hundreds of virtual machines. Simple, yet powerful; concise, yet robust; you will enjoy using this new language to solve your old problems using less code than you thought possible. If you are a system administrator responsible for managing a VMware Virtual Infrastructure (version 2.0 or above), or a standalone ESX Server (version 3.0 or above), then you need this book. Aimed at scripters of every level, the book starts off with a PowerShell primer and continues well into the internals of virtualization on the VMware platform. "

Getting Help

Windows PowerShell includes its own extensive, console-based help, reminiscent of man pages in Unix shells via the Get-Help cmdlet. This can be used to display both detailed information and examples for those times you are stuck with a cmdlet.

To use Get-help simply type get-help cmdlet as per the below example:

```
Get-Help Get-VM
```

Full detail can be gained by using:

```
Get-Help Get-VM -Detailed
```

Or just for the examples use:

```
Get-Help Get-VM -Examples
```

If you are still unsure then make sure you make use of the excellent PowerCLI community which can be accessed by typing Get-VIToolkitCommunity from the PowerCLI prompt, this includes the PowerCLI Blog, PowerCLI FAQ, PowerCLI Sample Code and a Q&A forum.

Virtualization EcoShell

So you can see the power behind both PowerShell and PowerCLI but are still not 100% sure you wish to delve into the shell just yet?

You can still utilize the full power in a nice graphical interface called Virtualization EcoShell.

The Virtualization EcoShell provides a simple, consistent, and integrated management user interface for creating, debugging and simplifying the management of Windows PowerShell scripts with robust scripting capabilities through an Integrated Development Environment (IDE) and best of all its completely free.

The Virtualization EcoShell once installed contains both a MMC style GUI with nodes, tasks and actions:

It also includes a fully functional Script Editor which can be used to debug and edit your code with auto-complete and color coded features:

Included are also multiple reporting features which utilize the full power of PowerCLI to generate customizable html, csv and Microsoft Visio outputted files:

An example HTML report:

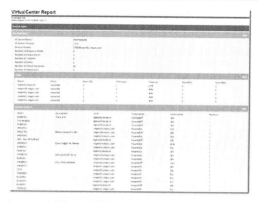

An example Microsoft Visio report:

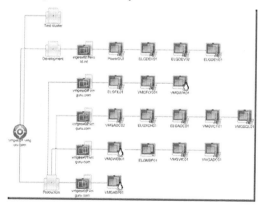

Download

This is a free application which can be downloaded from the following
URL: http://thevesi.org

Appendix A—Essential Commands

ESX Commands	
vdf	Displays the free disk space of all mounted devices known to the system (including VMkernel only devices) Options: -h human readable format (50G, 626M)
esxcli	Manages the Pluggable Storage Architecture
esxtop	Displays ESX system information
esxcfg-firewall	Used to configure the server's firewall
esxcfg-module	Manages the state of the driver modules loaded at boot
esxcfg-rescan	Forces the rescan of a VMkernel SCSI adapter (same as vmkfstools – rescan)
esxcfg-advcfg	Manages advanced configuration settings
esxcfg-vswitch	Command to manage virtual switches
esxcfg-info	Display the configuration of your ESX server
esxcfg-mpath	Manages the multi-pathing configuration of HBAs
esxcfg-resgrp	Manages resource groups on the ESX server
esxcfg-boot	Manages the GRUB boot loader
esxcfg-nas	Manages access to a Network Attached Storage (NAS) device
esxcfg-route	Manages the VMkernel default gateway
esxcfg-vmknic	Manages VMkernel associated network cards
esxcfg-nics	Manages speed and duplex settings for NICs
esxcfg-swiscsi	Manages the iSCSI software initiator
esxcfg-vswif	Manages the console NICs
vmkfstools	File system management tool
vmware-vim-cmd	Wrapper for "vimsh". Often used for fully automated scripted installations.

Linux Commands	
ls	Directory listing ls –las Options: -l list file and directory attributes -a do not hide entries starting with '.' -s print the size of each file -d list the names of directories -h print the output of file sizes in human readable format (e.g. 2.4G, 10M) -1 list one file per line (useful in shell scripts)
ll	Long list - short cut for ls –l
du	Estimates the space used by files

	du –ash /vmimages
	Options:
	-a include all files, not just directories
	-s display only the summary for each listed input
	-h display results in human readable format (1G, 258M)
	-c produce a grand total
df	Estimates the free space
	Options:
	-h display results in human readable format
dmesg	Displays what devices were found during boot
fdisk	Used to partition drives
ifconfig	Displays NIC information
ping	Used to send an ICMP message with the results echoed back.
traceroute	Displays the network path to a device
mke2fs	Creates a file system
tar	Creates a single file archive (tarball). When used with the –z option, the tarball is compressed with gzip.
cpio	Copy information to and from a tar file.
make	make uses a configuration file (Makefile) to read in parameters used in building software. Several scripts (Configure) are used to setup source code for the system that build is going to run on.
rpm	Red Hat's Package Manager. Used to install software.
	Options:
	-i Install a package
	-e remove a package
	-V verify packages installed (-Va for all)
	-q query for a package (-qf to display what package a file belongs to)
lsmod	Displays information about a module
modinfo	Prints information about a module
chown	Changes the ownership of a file
chmod	Changes permissions of a file or directory
chgrp	Changes group ownership
cat	View contents of a text file
tac	Review the contents of a text file in reverse
wc	Count the number of words in a text file
cp	Copy a file
mv	Move a file
rm	Remove a file
mkdir	Create a directory
rmdir	Remove a directory
pwd	Displays the current directory
ps	Display running process
top	Display system utilization

grep	Searches the contents of a file
find	Searches the file system for the name of a file
ln	Creates links (shortcuts) to files and directories
which	Searches your environment for the first occurrence of the given command
passwd	Change a users password
useradd	Adds a user to the system
userdel	Removes user from the system
groupadd	Creates a group
groupmod	Adds users to a group
lastlog	Displays when a user last logged onto the system
logger	Puts an entry into the messages log file
crontab	Displays jobs for a given user (crontab –e edits the crontab).
service	Starts or stops daemons (services)
chkconfig	Manages the runlevels of daemons (services)
man	Manual Pages for commands
	man which (displays how to use the which command)

Appendix B—Essential Utilities

The following table provides a list of essential tools that every ESX administrator should have available.

Tool Name	Description
PuTTY	Windows SSH client that allows connectivity to your ESX server. It can be found at: http://www.chiark.greenend.org.uk/~sgtatham/putty/
Winscp3	Windows SCP and SFTP client that allows you to securely copy files to your ESX server. Download WinSCP from here: http://winscp.net
Bart's PE	Bart's PE is utility to build yourself an OS on a disk. This is fully customizable and allows you to add drivers, plug-ins and applications: http://www.nu2.nu/pebuilder/
ucbd4win	Ultimate boot CD is a mixture of utilities built upon Bart's PE©. It is a life savior when doing P2V migrations: For more information: http://www.ubcd4win.com/
Ultimate P2V	Qui Hong , Chris Huss and Mike Laverick developed a process based on Bart's PE© to provide a free P2V framework. You can find it on Mike Laverick's site RTFM: http://www.rtfm-ed.co.uk/?page_id=174
OpenFiler	An open source NAS, virtual iSCSI target, and CIFS/SMB Linux distribution. This is greate for a lab environment. For more information: http://www.openfiler.com
Resource Pool Scheduler	Resource Pool Scheduler 1.2 is an application that is managed with a GUI but runs a service and is used to periodically change the settings of a vSphere Resource Pool: http://virtualizeplanet.com/mambo/index.php?option=com_content&task=view&id=59&Itemid=9
RVTools	RVTools is a freeware utility that assesses the environment on snapshots, attached ISOs, limits, reservations, disk space and more. It has a nice GUI and the ability to export to CSV. For more information: http://www.robware.net
vRanger Pro	vRanger Pro provides image-level hot backups of either the entire virtual machine or just a differential backup quickly and easily. Supporting VMware ESX and ESXi servers, vRanger Pro offers full VMware vCenter Server integration, is VMotion aware, and integrates with VCB: http://www.vizioncore.com/products/vRangerPro/

vFoglight Pro	vFoglight Pro is a best-in-class virtualization management solution that provides performance monitoring, capacity planning, and chargeback to help organizations mitigate the impact of resource sharing, optimize resource utilization, and recover infrastructure costs: http://www.vizioncore.com/products/vFoglight/
vControl	vControl is a VM management solution that provides self-service provisioning, multi-VM control and task-based automation. vControl lets VM consumers build and deploy VMs for themselves, while providing administrators a single interface for task-based administration of VMs. Furthermore, vControl allows organizations to automate manual and repetitive tasks, helping to reduce VM administration costs, improve management consistency and enabling a most cost-effective solution for high availability in the data center: http://www.vizioncore.com/products/vControl/
vConverter	vConverter is Vizioncore's P2V/V2V/V2P conversion solution that significantly reduces the time and effort spent converting servers to the VMware, Microsoft or Virtual Iron platforms. vConverter enables fast, easy and reliable conversions without disrupting the source physical system during the conversion process: http://www.vizioncore.com/products/vConverter/
vOptimizerPro	vOptimizer Pro is the only available storage optimization solution that finds and reclaims over-allocated VM storage and then realigns 64K partitions to optimize VM performance: http://www.vizioncore.com/products/vOptimizerPro/
vReplicator	vReplicator supports disaster recovery strategies with affordable replication of virtual servers: http://www.vizioncore.com/products/vReplicator/
Veeam Backup & Replication	Veeam Backup is the first enterprise-ready solution that combines backup and replication in a single product for fast recovery of your VMware ESX servers: http://www.veeam.com/vmware-esx-backup.html
Veeam FastSCP - Free	FastSCP provides a fast, secure and easy way to manage files and bulk copy VMs to your VMware ESX environment: http://www.veeam.com/vmware-esxi-fastscp.html
Veeam Reporter & Veeam Reporter Enterprise	Veeam Reporter Enterprise is the first reporting and change management solution specifically designed for large VMware Infrastructure 3 (VI3) virtual environments: http://www.veeam.com/vmware-esx-reporting_enterprise.html

Veeam Monitor & Veeam Monitor Free Edition	Veeam Monitor is an easy-to-deploy, framework-independent VMware monitoring solution designed to meet the day-to-day needs of VMware administrators: http://www.veeam.com/vmware-esx-monitoring.html
nworks Management Packs for MS and HP Operations Manager	The nworks Management Pack (MP) for VMware provides distributed monitoring and management of the VMware Infrastructure (VI) using Microsoft System Center Operations Manager 2007 and HP Operations Manager: http://www.veeam.com/vmware-microsoft-esx-monitoring.html
Veeam Configurator	Veeam Configurator 2.0 automatically discovers ESX and ESXi configurations across the enterprise and creates Veeam host profile templates. These templates can then be applied to groups of VMware hosts, and periodic scans can uncover inconsistencies and allow administrators to enforce defined templates to ensure policy compliance: http://www.veeam.com/vmware-esx-configure.html
Veeam RootAccess	The free Veeam RootAccess Wizard helps you enable or disable remote root access, or create a regular non-root user account which is not allowed by default on ESX Server. The newly created non-root user will belong to the default 'users' group and will be automatically granted remote SSH access. Su or sudo commands can then be used to elevate to the root account for privileged operations: http://www.veeam.com/root_access.html
vWire	vWire continuously monitors the state of virtual systems and correlates data with critical events to provide context and insight into potential issues, and then acts to prevent and resolve problems that cause downtime: http://www.vwire.com/
Tripwire ConfigCheck	A free utility that rapidly assesses the security of VMware ESX 3.0 and 3.5 hypervisor configurations compared to the VMware Infrastructure 3 Security Hardening guidelines: http://www.tripwire.com/configcheck/
OpsCheck	OpsCheck helps ensure your systems are configured to support VMware VMotion. OpsCheck rapidly analyzes ESX 3.0 and 3.5 and ESXi hypervisors, and provides troubleshooting guidance for VMware VMotion: http://www.vwire.com/free-tools/opscheck/
Hytrust Appliance	HyTrust provides a single point of control for hypervisor configuration, compliance, and access management that enables virtual infrastructure to become as operationally ready and secure as a physical infrastructure: http://www.hytrust.com
PHD	Several great tools including Snaphunter (identify open snapshots), KS Quickconfig (installation automation)

and VMNetBac (export your VM network configuration):
http://www.phdvirtual.com/component/jdownloads/?task=viewcategory&catid=3

Hyper9

Hyper9 offers solutions that help virtualization infrastructure administrators manage their environment. Hyper9 is a simple, yet powerful enterprise-class product that helps VI administrators manage virtual server infrastructures without agents, tree views, spreadsheets, or multiple tools, and it enables monitoring, troubleshooting and reporting on virtual infrastructures:
http://www.hyper9.com/product_overview.aspx

Appendix C—PowerCLI Cmdlets

The following table provides a list of all PowerCLI cmdlets as of version 4.0.0 | Build 162509

Name	Description
Add-VMHost	Adds a virtual machine host to be managed by the VMM server.
Add-VMHostNtpServer	Adds the specified NTP servers to the NTP server list of the specified hosts.
Apply-VMHostProfile	Applies a virtual machine host profile to the specified entity.
Connect-VIServer	Connects to a vSphere server.
Disconnect-VIServer	Disconnects from a vSphere server.
Dismount-Tools	Dismounts the VMware Tools installer CD.
Export-VMHostProfile	Exports the specified virtual machine host profile to a file.
Get-CDDrive	Gets the status from a virtual machine, template or snapshot of one or more virtual CD drives.
Get-Cluster	Gets from a vSphere server one or more clusters.
Get-Datacenter	Gets from a vSphere server one or more datacenters.
Get-Datastore	Gets from a vSphere server one or more datastores.
Get-DrsRule	Retrieves the list of DRS rules for the specified clusters.
Get-FloppyDrive	Gets the status from a virtual machine, template or snapshot of one or more virtual floppy drives.
Get-Folder	Gets from a vSphere server one or more folders.
Get-HardDisk	Gets from a vSphere server one or more virtual hard disks.
Get-Inventory	Gets from a vSphere server objects that represent inventory items.
Get-Log	Retrieves entries from vSphere logs.
Get-LogType	Gets information about the available logs on a virtual machine host.
Get-NetworkAdapter	Gets from a vSphere server one or more virtual network adapters.
Get-OSCustomizationSpec	Gets from a vSphere server available OS customization specifications.
Get-ResourcePool	Gets from a vSphere server one or more resource pools.

Get-ScsiLun	Retrieves SCSI devices from the specified virtual machine host(s).
Get-ScsiLunPath	Retrieves the list of vmhba paths to a specified SCSI device.
Get-Snapshot	Gets from a vSphere server one or more virtual machine snapshots.
Get-Stat	Gets statistical information from vSphere servers.
Get-StatInterval	Retrieves the available statistics intervals and filters them using the provided parameters.
Get-StatType	Retrieves the available statistics types for a given inventory object.
Get-Task	Gets from a vSphere server one or more tasks.
Get-Template	Gets from a vSphere server one or more virtual machine templates.
Get-VICredentialStoreItem	Retrieves credential store items.
Get-VIEvent	Gets event information from a vSphere server.
Get-View	Returns a vSphere .Net view object by specified search criteria.
Get-VIObjectByVIView	Converts a vSphere .Net View object to a PowerShell VIObject based on ID.
Get-VirtualPortGroup	Gets port groups for hosts, virtual machines, or virtual switches.
Get-VirtualSwitch	Gets the virtual switches configured for a host or used by a virtual machine.
Get-VIToolkitConfiguration	Gets the vSphere PowerCLI proxy configuration.
Get-VIToolkitVersion	Gets the VMware vSphere PowerCLI version.
Get-VM	Gets from a vSphere server one or more virtual machines.
Get-VMGuest	Gets from a vSphere server one or more virtual machine guests.
Get-VMHost	Gets from a vSphere server one or more virtual machine hosts.
Get-VMHostAccount	Retrieves the host accounts from one or more vSphere servers.
Get-VMHostAdvancedConfiguration	Retrieves the advanced configuration of the specified virtual machine host.
Get-VMHostDiagnosticPartition	Retrieves a list of diagnostic partitions for the specified virtual machine hosts.
Get-VMHostFirewallDefaultPolicy	Gets the firewall default policy for the specified virtual machine hosts.
Get-VMHostFirewallException	Retrieves the firewall exceptions for the specified virtual machine hosts.

Get-VMHostFirmware	Retrieves the virtual machine host's firmware information.
Get-VMHostModule	Retrieves the option strings of the specified virtual machine host modules.
Get-VMHostNetwork	Gets from a vSphere server one or more virtual machine host networks.
Get-VMHostNtpServer	Retrieves the NTP servers of the specified virtual machine hosts.
Get-VMHostProfile	Retrieves a virtual machine host profile.
Get-VMHostService	Gets information of a virtual machine host service.
Get-VMHostSnmp	Retrieves the virtual machine host's SNMP configuration.
Get-VMHostStartPolicy	Retrieves the start policy of the specified virtual machine hosts.
Get-VMHostStorage	Gets from a vSphere server one or more storage adapters.
Get-VMHostSysLogServer	Displays the remote syslog servers of the specified hosts.
Get-VMResourceConfiguration	Retrieves information about resource allocation between the virtual machines.
Get-VMStartPolicy	Gets the start policies of virtual machines.
Import-VMHostProfile	Imports a virtual machine host profile from file. The file path must be accessible from the vSphere PowerCLI client side.
Invoke-VMScript	Executes the specified PowerShell script in the guest OS of each of the specified virtual machines.
Mount-Tools	Mounts the VMware Tools CD installer as a CD-ROM for the guest operating system.
Move-Cluster	Moves a vSphere cluster from one location to another.
Move-Datacenter	Moves a vSphere datacenter from one location to another.
Move-Folder	Moves a vSphere folder from one location to another.
Move-Inventory	Moves a vSphere inventory item from one location to another.
Move-ResourcePool	Moves a resource pool from one location to another.
Move-VM	Moves a virtual machine from one location to another.
Move-VMHost	Moves a virtual machine host from one location to another.
New-CDDrive	Creates a new virtual CD drive.
New-Cluster	Creates a new cluster.

New-CustomField	Creates a new custom field for a particular inventory item type.
New-Datacenter	Creates a new datacenter.
New-Datastore	Creates a new datastore.
New-DrsRule	Creates a new DRS rule.
New-FloppyDrive	Creates a new virtual floppy drive.
New-Folder	Creates a new folder on a vSphere server.
New-HardDisk	Creates a new hard disk for the specified virtual machine.
New-NetworkAdapter	Creates a new virtual network adapter.
New-OSCustomizationSpec	Creates a new OS customization specification.
New-ResourcePool	Creates a new resource pool.
New-Snapshot	Creates a new snapshot on a virtual machine.
New-StatInterval	Creates a statistics interval with the specified parameters.
New-Template	Creates a new template.
New-VICredentialStoreItem	Creates a new entry in the credential store.
New-VirtualPortGroup	Creates a new port group on the specified host.
New-VirtualSwitch	Creates a new virtual switch.
New-VM	Creates a new virtual machine.
New-VMHostAccount	Creates a new virtual machine host user or group account.
New-VMHostNetworkAdapter	Creates a new Service Console or VMkernel portgroup on the specified virtual machine host.
New-VMHostProfile	Creates a new virtual machine host profile based on a reference host.
Remove-CDDrive	Removes virtual CD drives from the specified targets.
Remove-Cluster	Deletes the specified cluster or clusters.
Remove-CustomField	Deletes the specified custom field for a specified type of inventory item.
Remove-Datacenter	Removes the specified datacenter or datacenters from their locations.
Remove-Datastore	Removes the specified datastore or datastores from their locations.
Remove-DrsRule	Removes the specified DRS rules.
Remove-FloppyDrive	Removes virtual floppy drives from the specified targets.
Remove-Folder	Removes the specified folder or folders

	from their locations.
Remove-Inventory	Removes the specified inventory item or items from their locations.
Remove-NetworkAdapter	Removes virtual network adapters from their locations.
Remove-OSCustomizationSpec	Removes the specified OS customization specification(s).
Remove-ResourcePool	Removes the specified resource pool or resource pools from their locations.
Remove-Snapshot	Removes the specified virtual machine snapshot or snapshots.
Remove-StatInterval	Removes the statistics interval specified by the provided sampling period or name.
Remove-Template	Removes the specified virtual machine template or templates.
Remove-VICredentialStoreItem	Removes the specified credential store items.
Remove-VirtualPortGroup	Removes a virtual port group.
Remove-VirtualSwitch	Removes the virtual switches from their locations.
Remove-VM	Removes the specified virtual machines from the vSphere server.
Remove-VMHost	Removes the virtual machine host from the vCenter Server inventory ending its management.
Remove-VMHostAccount	Removes the specified host accounts.
Remove-VMHostNetworkAdapter	Removes the specified NIC(s).
Remove-VMHostNtpServer	Removes the specified NTP servers from the NTP server list of the specified hosts.
Remove-VMHostProfile	Removes the specified virtual machine host profile.
Restart-VMGuest	Restarts the virtual machine guest operating system.
Restart-VMHostService	Restarts the specified virtual machine host services.
Set-CDDrive	Changes the configuration of a virtual CD drive.
Set-Cluster	Changes the configuration of a cluster.
Set-CustomField	Sets the value of a custom field for a particular inventory item.
Set-Datacenter	Changes the name of the datacenter.
Set-Datastore	Changes the name of the datastore.
Set-DrsRule	Modifies an existing DRS rule.
Set-FloppyDrive	Changes the configuration of a virtual floppy drive.

Set-Folder	Changes the name of a folder.
Set-HardDisk	Updates the specified virtual hard disk.
Set-NetworkAdapter	Changes the configuration of a virtual network adapter.
Set-OSCustomizationSpec	Updates the specified OS customization specification(s).
Set-ResourcePool	Changes the configuration of a resource pool.
Set-ScsiLun	Configures a SCSI device.
Set-ScsiLunPath	Configures a vmhba path to a SCSI device.
Set-Snapshot	Changes the name and/or description of the virtual machine snapshot.
Set-StatInterval	Updates the statistics interval specified by the provided parameters.
Set-Template	Changes the name and/or the description of a virtual machine template.
Set-VirtualPortGroup	Updates the specified virtual port group.
Set-VirtualSwitch	Updates the properties of a specified virtual switch.
Set-VIToolkitConfiguration	Sets the vSphere PowerCLI proxy configuration.
Set-VM	Changes the configuration of a virtual machine.
Set-VMHost	Changes the configuration of a virtual machine host.
Set-VMHostAccount	Updates a virtual machine host account.
Set-VMHostAdvancedConfiguration	Updates the advanced configuration settings of one or more virtual machine hosts.
Set-VMHostDiagnosticPartition	Activates or deactivates the diagnostic partitions of virtual machine hosts.
Set-VMHostFirewallDefaultPolicy	Sets the default firewall policy for the specified virtual machine host.
Set-VMHostFirewallException	Enables or disables a virtual machine host's firewall exceptions.
Set-VMHostFirmware	Sets the host's firmware.
Set-VMHostModule	Overrides the host's module options with the specified ones.
Set-VMHostNetwork	Updates the specified virtual network.
Set-VMHostNetworkAdapter	Updates the specified virtual machine hosts network adapter.
Set-VMHostProfile	Modifies the specified virtual machine host profile.
Set-VMHostService	Updates a virtual machine host service.

Set-VMHostSnmp	Updates the host's SNMP configuration.
Set-VMHostStartPolicy	Updates the host's default start policy.
Set-VMHostSysLogServer	Configures the remote syslog server for the specified hosts.
Set-VMResourceConfiguration	Configures resource allocation between the virtual machines.
Set-VMStartPolicy	Updates the start policy for the specified virtual machines.
Shutdown-VMGuest	Shutdowns the specified virtual machine guest OS.
Start-VM	Powers on one or more virtual machines.
Start-VMHostService	Starts the specified virtual machine host services.
Stop-Task	Stops the specified task or tasks.
Stop-VM	Powers off one or more virtual machines.
Stop-VMHostService	Stops a virtual machine host service.
Suspend-VM	Suspends a virtual machine.
Suspend-VMGuest	Suspends a virtual machine guest OS.
Test-VMHostProfileCompliance	Tests virtual machine hosts for profile compliance.
Test-VMHostSnmp	Tests the host's SNMP configuration.
Update-Tools	Upgrades VMware Tools on the specified virtual machines.
Wait-Task	Waits for the completion of the specified task or tasks.

About the Authors

 Bernie Baker is a Sr. VMware Specialist and is a member of EMC's VMware Affinity Team working under the guidance of Chad Sakac (virtualgeek.typepad.com). The VMware Affinity Team is responsible for all of EMC's VMware focused activities, including the overall strategic alliance, joint engineering projects, joint reference architectures and solutions validation, joint services, marketing activity and sales engagement across global geographies.

Bernie has been involved in the computer industry since 1987 and has worked for a number of tier-1 organizations including Dell, Inc. and VMware. During his tenure, Bernie has worked in various technological capacities as an individual contributor and as a member of engineering management teams. He has been working with EMC and VMware solutions since 1999. In his current capacity, Bernie is focused on cooperative technology solutions from EMC, VMware and Cisco.

Bernie attended college at Northeastern University and Wentworth Institute of Technology where he studied Computer Engineering and Computer Science.

 Thomas Bryant is the Director of Advanced Technology & Products for Vizioncore. His primary focus is on the strategic planning & rapid application development of the next generation of virtualization solutions. With over 14 of years experience in Management & Information Technology, Thomas has a broad-based background including holding key industry certifications & recognitions from VMware, Microsoft and Citrix. Thomas also devotes his time to sharing knowledge with the community by speaking at industry events, posting on community forums and being a moderator for various groups including the VMware Communities. Thomas maintains his popular blog at http://blog.thb3.com.

 Duncan Epping is a Senior Consultant and the EMEA Datacenter Practice Lead working for VMware PSO. He works with enterprise customers primarily focused on designing virtual infrastructures and BC-DR. Duncan is a VMware Certified Professional and a VMware Certified Design Expert (VCDX 007). He is the owner of Yellow-Bricks.com, one of the leading VMware / virtualization blogs worldwide and an active contributor and moderator on the VMTN Community forums.

Dave Mishchenko has been in the IT industry for 12 years. He is currently a Senior Technical Analyst with Agresso Corporation a leading ERP provider. Dave provides technical leadership for Agresso's hosting and ASP services. He also provides consulting services to Agresso's customers and focuses on network infrastructure and security, thin client computing, database tuning, server hardware and virtualization. Dave is actively involved in the VMware Community forums where he is a user moderator and in particular focuses on VMware ESXi.

Dave resides in Vancouver, Canda with his wife Marcia and four children: Karis, Luke, Ariana and Yerik. When not on VMware's forums or maintaining www.vm-help.com, he can be found wakeboarding with his family at one of the local lakes. Dave holds a degree in Mechanical Engineering from the University of Western Ontario, Canada.

Stuart Radnidge has been designing virtual infrastructures for large enterprises in the finance industry for several years. He left his home of Sydney, Australia with dreams of moving to Japan and becoming a Ninja, but somehow ended up living in London and working for a Tier 1 global investment bank. He likes life, wife, travel, gaming and swearing in public via his blog at vinternals.com.

Alan Renouf is an independent consultant currently working for a large local government organisation in the UK. He has been working with VMware, Citrix and Microsoft products for a number of years. In the last few years he has concentrated on virtualisation products and the automation of these using PowerShell. Alan is a keen blogger (http://virtu-al.net) and the co-host of the Get-Scripting podcast which is a podcast dedicated to the world of all that is PowerShell related - you can find this at http://get-scripting.blogspot.com. You can also follow Alan on Twitter at http://twitter.com/alanrenouf.